JUSTFOUR
Ingredients

THE AUSTRALIAN
Women's Weekly

JUSTFOUR
Ingredients

acp books

34

Brunch

It's the weekend. Time to sleep in and enjoy a slower pace. Spread the newspaper over the table or invite friends around. Brunch is a meal to linger over – there's no need to rush.

rhubarb, muesli and yogurt cups

2 cups (220g) coarsely chopped
    fresh or frozen rhubarb
¼ cup (55g) caster sugar
1⅓ cups (375g) low-fat
    vanilla yogurt
⅓ cup (50g) toasted muesli

preparation and cooking time
20 minutes (plus refrigeration time)
serves 4
nutritional count per serving
1.5g total fat (0.5g saturated fat);
782kJ (187 cal); 33.9g carbohydrate;
7.4g protein; 2.9g fibre

1 Combine rhubarb, sugar and ½ cup water
in medium saucepan; bring to the boil. Reduce
heat; simmer, uncovered, stirring occasionally,
about 10 minutes or until rhubarb is tender.
Transfer to medium heatproof bowl, cover;
refrigerate 1 hour.
2 Divide mixture among four ¾-cup (180ml)
serving glasses; top with yogurt then muesli.

strawberries and mint in orange syrup

1 medium orange (240g)
2 tablespoons grated palm sugar
500g quartered strawberries
¼ cup coarsely chopped
    fresh mint

preparation and cooking time
10 minutes
serves 4
nutritional count per serving
0.2g total fat (0g saturated fat);
305kJ (73 cal); 13.2g carbohydrate;
2.7g protein; 3.8g fibre

1 Grate rind from orange (you need 2 teaspoons);
juice orange (you need 2 tablespoons).
2 Stir palm sugar and ¼ cup water in small
saucepan, over low heat, until sugar dissolves;
bring to the boil. Boil, uncovered, without stirring,
about 3 minutes or until syrup thickens slightly.
Remove from heat.
3 Stir rind and juice into syrup; cool. Combine
strawberries and mint in medium bowl with
syrup. Divide among serving dishes; serve with
crème fraîche, if desired.

tip Make the rhubarb the day before, if you like. Keep it, covered, in the fridge, so all you have to do is spoon everything into the serving glasses. Rhubarb stalks are the only edible portion of the plant – the leaves contain a toxic substance and should not be eaten.

tip These days many berries come packaged in clear plastic containers. Turn the container over and check the berries at bottom as they can become mouldy. Berries don't ripen once they're picked, so the deeply coloured ones tend to be the sweetest and most flavourful.

pancakes

1 cup (150g) self-raising flour
¼ cup (55g) caster sugar
2 eggs
1 cup (250ml) milk

preparation and cooking time
25 minutes
serves 4
nutritional count per serving
5.5g total fat (2.5g saturated fat);
1104kJ (264 cal); 43.3g carbohydrate;
9.1g protein; 1.4g fibre

1 Sift flour and sugar into medium bowl; gradually whisk in combined eggs and milk, whisking until batter is smooth.
2 Pour ¼ cup batter into heated oiled medium frying pan; cook pancake until bubbles begin to appear on surface. Turn pancake; cook until browned lightly. Cover to keep warm.
3 Repeat with remaining batter.
4 Serve pancakes with your choice of topping, or try one of the toppings, below.

rhubarb and pear compote

preparation and cooking time
10 minutes
serves 4
nutritional count per serving
0.2g total fat (0g saturated fat);
380kJ (91 cal); 19.8g carbohydrate;
1g protein; 2.7g fibre

Combine 2 cups coarsely chopped rhubarb, 1 coarsely chopped medium pear, ¼ cup caster sugar, 1 teaspoon mixed spice and 2 tablespoons water in medium saucepan; bring to the boil. Reduce heat; simmer, stirring occasionally, about 5 minutes or until fruit softens slightly.

berries with vanilla syrup

preparation and cooking time
10 minutes
serves 4
nutritional count per serving
0.1g total fat (0g saturated fat);
309kJ (74 cal); 15.7g carbohydrate;
1.4g protein; 2g fibre

Combine ¼ cup water and ¼ cup caster sugar in small saucepan. Split one vanilla bean lengthways; scrape seeds into saucepan. Stir over low heat until sugar dissolves. Bring to the boil; boil, uncovered, without stirring, about 3 minutes or until syrup thickens slightly. Stir in 300g frozen mixed berries and ¼ cup coarsely chopped fresh mint.

honeyed ricotta and pears

825g can sliced pears, drained,
  sliced thickly
1 cup (240g) reduced-fat
  ricotta cheese
2 tablespoons honey
¼ teaspoon finely grated
  orange rind

preparation and cooking time
10 minutes
serves 4
nutritional count per serving
5.2g total fat (3.4g saturated fat);
715kJ (171 cal); 22.8g carbohydrate;
7g protein; 2g fibre

1 Preheat grill.
2 Place pears on oven tray; grill 5 minutes or until browned lightly.
3 Combine cheese, honey and rind in small bowl. Serve pears topped with cheese mixture. Serve with toasted fruit bread, if desired.

baked eggs with pancetta

6 slices pancetta (90g),
  chopped finely
4 green onions, chopped finely
²/₃ cup (50g) finely grated
  parmesan cheese
8 eggs

preparation and cooking time
20 minutes
serves 4
nutritional count per serving
17.7g total fat (7g saturated fat);
1053kJ (252 cal); 0.9g carbohydrate;
22.6g protein; 0.2g fibre

1 Preheat oven to 200°C/180°C fan-forced. Lightly oil four ¾-cup (180ml) ovenproof dishes.
2 Cook pancetta in heated oiled medium frying pan until crisp. Add onion; cook, stirring, until onion just softens. Remove from heat; stir in half the cheese.
3 Divide pancetta mixture among dishes; break two eggs into each dish. Bake, uncovered, in oven, 5 minutes. Sprinkle remaining cheese over eggs; return to oven. Bake, uncovered, 5 minutes or until eggs are just set. Serve immediately.

tip Doongara rice is Australian developed and grown. It's a white, long-grain rice similar to basmati, and has a higher content of amylose (starch) than other rice, which means it is more slowly digested – it has a lower glycaemic index than most other rice varieties.

tip Baby spinach is sold in containers of loose leaves rather than in bunches. The leaves are tender and sweet and are the perfect complement to the velvety texture of the egg.

rice porridge with raisins

½ cup (100g) doongara rice
2⅔ cups (660ml) skim milk
1 tablespoon brown sugar
¼ cup (40g) raisins

preparation and cooking time
40 minutes
serves 4
nutritional count per serving
0.4g total fat (0.2g saturated fat);
811kJ (194 cal); 38.6g carbohydrate;
8.1g protein; 0.7g fibre
If you cannot find doongara rice, use
white long-grain rice, instead.

1 Combine rice and ½ cup water in small saucepan; bring to the boil. Reduce heat; simmer, uncovered, until liquid is absorbed.
2 Add 2 cups of the milk, sugar and raisins; simmer about 20 minutes or until rice is tender, stirring occasionally. Serve warm with remaining milk.

breakfast with the lot

2 large egg tomatoes (180g),
    quartered
4 eggs
60g light ham
50g baby spinach leaves

preparation and cooking time
35 minutes
serves 4
nutritional count per serving
5.9g total fat (1.8g saturated fat);
418kJ (106 cal); 1.3g carbohydrate;
16.2g protein; 1g fibre

1 Preheat oven to 220°C/200°C fan-forced. Line oven tray with baking paper.
2 Place tomato, cut-side up, on oven tray; roast about 25 minutes or until softened and browned lightly.
3 Meanwhile, place enough water in large shallow frying pan to come halfway up the side; bring to the boil. Break one egg into a cup then slide egg into pan; repeat with remaining eggs. Allow water to return to the boil. Cover pan, turn off heat; stand about 4 minutes or until a light film of egg white has set over each yolk.
4 Using an egg slide, remove eggs, one at a time, from pan; place egg, still on slide, on absorbent-paper-lined saucer to blot up any poaching liquid. Serve ham, spinach, egg and tomato with toasted grain bread, if desired.

cheese and corn omelettes

Add a bit of crisp bacon or even a few pan-fried mushrooms to the omelette, if you like.

8 eggs
310g can creamed corn
¼ cup finely chopped fresh
   flat-leaf parsley
½ cup (60g) coarsely grated
   reduced-fat cheddar cheese

preparation and cooking time
30 minutes
serves 4
nutritional count per serving
14.6g total fat (5.6g saturated fat);
1112kJ (266 cal); 13.2g carbohydrate;
19.2g protein; 2.8g fibre

1 Whisk eggs in medium bowl until combined; stir in remaining ingredients.
2 Pour a quarter of the egg mixture into heated oiled small frying pan; cook over medium heat until omelette is set. Fold omelette in half, slide onto plate; cover to keep warm.
3 Repeat process with remaining egg mixture to make four omelettes.

bacon and asparagus frittata

4 rindless bacon rashers (260g),
   sliced thickly
170g asparagus, trimmed,
   halved lengthways
6 eggs
¾ cup (180ml) buttermilk

preparation and cooking time
50 minutes
serves 4
nutritional count per serving
17.5g total fat (6.2g saturated fat);
1137kJ (272 cal); 3.4g carbohydrate;
25.2g protein; 0.4g fibre

1 Preheat oven to 180°C/160°C fan-forced. Oil deep 19cm-square cake pan; line base and sides with baking paper.
2 Cook bacon, stirring, in heated small frying pan until crisp; drain on absorbent paper. Layer bacon and asparagus in prepared pan.
3 Whisk eggs and buttermilk in medium jug; pour into pan. Bake, uncovered, in oven, about 35 minutes or until frittata is set. Stand 10 minutes before cutting into squares.

eggs with tomato and basil

2 tablespoons olive oil

1kg egg tomatoes,
    chopped coarsely

1 cup coarsely chopped fresh basil

8 eggs

preparation and cooking time
20 minutes
serves 4
nutritional count per serving
3.8g total fat (4.5g saturated fat);
1141kJ (273 cal); 6.2g carbohydrate;
15.9g protein; 3.8g fibre

1 Heat oil in large frying pan; cook tomato, stirring, 10 minutes or until thick and pulpy. Stir in basil.

2 Using medium shallow mixing spoon, make eight shallow depressions into tomato mixture. Break one egg into a cup, then slide egg into one of the hollows in tomato mixture. Repeat with remaining eggs. Cover pan; cook over low heat about 5 minutes or until eggs are just set.

3 Use egg slide to carefully lift egg and tomato mixture onto each serving plate. Serve with crusty bread, if desired.

huevos rancheros

1 small red onion (100g),
    chopped finely

400g can mexican-flavoured
    chopped tomatoes

4 eggs

4 corn tortillas, warmed

preparation and cooking time
30 minutes
serves 4
nutritional count per serving
5.9g total fat (1.7g saturated fat);
602kJ (144 cal); 12.5g carbohydrate;
8.9g protein; 2.5g fibre
If you can't find mexican-flavoured tomatoes, use a can of chopped tomatoes with add a dash of chilli sauce.

1 Cook onion in heated oiled large frying pan, stirring, until softened. Add tomatoes; bring to the boil. Reduce heat; simmer, uncovered, 10 minutes, stirring occasionally, or until thickened.

2 Using medium shallow mixing spoon, make four shallow depressions into tomato mixture. Break one egg into a cup then slide egg into one of the hollows in tomato mixture; repeat with remaining eggs. Cover pan; cook over low heat, about 5 minutes or until eggs are just set.

3 Divide warmed tortillas among plates. Use egg slide to carefully lift egg and tomato mixture onto each tortilla.

poached eggs with bacon and pecorino

600g spinach, trimmed,
    chopped coarsely
4 rindless bacon rashers (260g)
4 eggs
⅓ cup (40g) shaved pecorino cheese

preparation and cooking time
15 minutes
serves 4
nutritional count per serving
16.9g total fat (6.5g saturated fat);
1062kJ (254 cal); 0.9g carbohydrate;
23.9g protein; 2.1g fibre

1 Boil, steam or microwave spinach until just wilted; drain. Cover to keep warm.
2 Meanwhile, cook bacon in heated large frying pan until crisp. Drain on absorbent paper; cover to keep warm.
3 Half-fill same pan with water; bring to the boil. Break one egg into a cup then slide into pan. When all eggs are in pan, allow water to return to the boil. Cover pan, turn off heat; stand about 4 minutes or until a light film of egg white sets over yolks. Remove eggs from pan, one at a time, using slotted spoon; place on absorbent-paper-lined saucer to blot up poaching liquid.
4 Divide spinach among serving plates; top with bacon, egg then cheese.

egg-white omelette

We used chives, chervil and parsley in this recipe.

12 egg whites
1 cup finely chopped fresh
    mixed herbs
½ cup (60g) coarsely grated
    cheddar cheese
½ cup (50g) coarsely grated
    mozzarella cheese

preparation and cooking time
45 minutes
serves 4
nutritional count per serving
8g total fat (5.1g saturated fat);
614kJ (147 cal); 0.5g carbohydrate;
17.9g protein; 0.7g fibre

1 Preheat grill.
2 Beat a quarter of the egg white in small bowl with electric mixer until soft peaks form; fold in a quarter of the herbs.
3 Pour mixture into heated oiled 20cm-frying pan; cook, uncovered, over low heat until omelette is just browned lightly on the bottom.
4 Preheat grill. Sprinkle a quarter of the combined cheeses over half the omelette. Place pan under grill until cheese begins to melt and omelette sets; fold omelette over to completely cover cheese. Carefully slide onto serving plate; cover to keep warm.
5 Repeat process with remaining egg white, herbs and cheese to make three more omelettes.

tip Make sure you time the poaching of the eggs. Ideally, you want the egg yolk to be runny and starting to harden around the edges. It will burst open when you cut it, adding to the wonderful combination of flavours and textures.

tip The magic of this omelette lies in its light, fluffy texture. Be sure to beat the egg whites thoroughly and watch the pan under the griller with an eagle eye so the omelette doesn't overcook.

baked ricotta with spinach

100g baby spinach leaves
1¼ cups (250g) low-fat
  ricotta cheese
1 egg, beaten lightly
2 tablespoons coarsely chopped
  fresh garlic chives

preparation and cooking time
20 minutes
serves 4
nutritional count per serving
6.8g total fat (3.9g saturated fat);
435kJ (104 cal); 1.6g carbohydrate;
8.8g protein; 0.7g fibre

1 Preheat oven to 200°C/180°C fan-forced.
Oil four holes of a six-hole (1/3-cup/80ml)
muffin pan.
2 Cook spinach in heated oiled large frying pan
until wilted. Cool.
3 Combine spinach in medium bowl with cheese,
egg and chives; divide among prepared pan holes.
Bake, uncovered, in oven, about 15 minutes or
until browned lightly. Serve baked ricotta with
toasted ciabatta bread, if desired.

baked beans, bacon, tomato and chives

2 medium tomatoes (300g),
  chopped coarsely
1 tablespoon finely chopped
  fresh chives
420g can baked beans in
  tomato sauce
4 rindless bacon rashers (260g),
  chopped coarsely

preparation and cooking time
10 minutes
serves 4
nutritional count per serving
8.6g total fat (2.9g saturated fat);
886kJ (212 cal); 13.5g carbohydrate;
17.2g protein; 6g fibre

1 Combine tomato and chives in small bowl.
2 Heat beans in small saucepan.
3 Meanwhile, cook bacon, stirring, in heated
small frying pan until crisp; drain on absorbent
paper. Serve beans and bacon topped with
tomato mixture. Serve with toasted turkish or
ciabatta bread, if you like.

cheesy scrambled eggs with spinach

8 eggs
⅓ cup (80g) reduced-fat
   spreadable cream cheese
50g baby spinach leaves,
   chopped coarsely

preparation and cooking time
10 minutes
serves 4
nutritional count per serving
13.8g total fat (5.4g saturated fat);
790kJ (189 cal); 1g carbohydrate;
15.3g protein; 0.3g fibre

1 Whisk eggs in medium bowl until combined then whisk in cheese and spinach.
2 Cook mixture, stirring gently, in heated oiled large frying pan, over low heat, until almost set. Serve with wholemeal toast, if you like.

pumpkin and zucchini frittata

500g butternut pumpkin,
   chopped coarsely
2 large zucchini (300g),
   chopped coarsely
8 eggs
½ cup (125ml) cream

preparation and cooking time
1 hour 20 minutes
serves 4
nutritional count per serving
24.6g total fat (12.5g saturated fat);
1371kJ (328 cal); 9g carbohydrate;
17g protein; 2.4g fibre

1 Preheat oven to 200°C/180°C fan-forced. Oil and line base and side of deep 22cm-round cake pan with baking paper.
2 Combine pumpkin and zucchini, in single layer, in large baking dish; spray with cooking-oil spray. Roast about 30 minutes or until vegetables are tender and brown; place in prepared pan.
3 Reduce oven temperature to 160°C/140°C fan-forced.
4 Whisk eggs in medium bowl until frothy. Whisk in cream; pour over vegetables. Bake, uncovered, about 40 minutes or until frittata sets and is just cooked through.

tip Mascarpone is not for the diet conscious. It's a triple-cream cheese made from cows milk, and is one of the key ingredients in the Italian dessert Tiramisu.

tip You can find belgian-style waffles on supermarkets shelves and at most delicatessens. They are a thick, crispy and fluffy waffle made with a yeast batter.

mixed berry and mascarpone brioche

1 cup (250ml) thickened cream
200g mascarpone cheese
4 thick slices brioche
250g mixed fresh berries

preparation and cooking time
10 minutes
serves 4
nutritional count per serving
56.1g total fat (35.6g saturated fat);
2985kJ (714 cal); 41.5g carbohydrate;
10.9g protein; 2.6g fibre

1 Beat cream in small bowl with electric mixer until soft peaks form; fold in cheese.
2 Preheat grill. Toast brioche, both sides, under grill. Place one brioche slice on each serving plate; spread with cheese mixture then top with berries. Serve sprinkled with a little finely chopped fresh mint and dust with sifted icing sugar, if you like.

waffles with maple syrup and strawberries

8 packaged belgian-style
    waffles (400g)
20g butter
500g strawberries, sliced thickly
½ cup (125ml) pure maple syrup

preparation and cooking time
25 minutes
serves 4
nutritional count per serving
22.8g total fat (10.4g saturated fat);
2341kJ (560 cal); 73.5g carbohydrate;
12.4g protein; 4.9g fibre

1 Preheat oven to 160°C/140°C fan-forced.
2 Place waffles, in single layer, on oven tray; heat, uncovered, about 8 minutes.
3 Meanwhile, melt butter in medium frying pan, add strawberries; cook, stirring gently, about 2 minutes or until just heated through. Add maple syrup; cook, stirring gently, until heated through.
4 Divide waffles among serving plates; top with strawberry-maple mixture and a dollop of plain yogurt or thickened cream, if desired.

34

Snacks + Light Meals

Whipping up a quick or light meal doesn't mean you have to sacrifice taste or nutrition. Here are some palate-pleasing options to expand your repertoire of simple meals.

bruschetta caprese

½ long loaf turkish bread (215g)

250g cherry tomatoes,
   sliced thickly

100g baby bocconcini cheese,
   sliced thickly

1 cup loosely packed fresh
   basil leaves

1 Preheat grill.

2 Cut bread crossways into four even pieces;
split each piece horizontally. Toast bread, cut-
sides up, under grill.

3 Place two slices toast on each serving plate.
Top with tomato, cheese and basil; drizzle with
extra virgin olive oil, if desired.

preparation and cooking time
15 minutes

serves 4

nutritional count per serving
5.7g total fat (2.8g saturated fat);
828kJ (198 cal); 25.5g carbohydrate;
9.5g protein; 2.7g fibre

tomato, spinach and cheese muffin

60g baby spinach leaves

2 medium tomatoes (300g),
   sliced thickly

⅔ cup (80g) coarsely grated
   cheddar cheese

4 english muffins, split (260g)

1 Preheat grill.

2 Layer spinach, tomato and cheese on muffins.
Place muffins on oven tray; heat under grill until
cheese is melted.

preparation and cooking time
15 minutes

serves 4

nutritional count per serving
7.8g total fat (4.5g saturated fat);
949kJ (227 cal); 24.9g carbohydrate;
12.5g protein; 3.2g fibre

tip Layer your ingredients carefully and artfully into a colourful little stack. The baby bocconcini is sold in supermarkets, in tubs of brine or water.

tip Like bread, muffins can be frozen so you can always have them in fresh supply. It's a good idea to cut them in half before you freeze them so they are ready to use when you take them out of the freezer rather than having to wait for them to defrost.

watercress and yogurt dip

1 cup loosely packed
  fresh watercress
1 teaspoon ground cumin
¼ teaspoon cayenne pepper
1 cup (280g) yogurt

preparation time 5 minutes
makes 1 cup
nutritional count per ¼ cup
2.4g total fat (1.5g saturated fat);
222kJ (53 cal); 3.4g carbohydrate;
3.6g protein; 0.4g fibre

1 Blend or process watercress, spices and
2 tablespoons of the yogurt until smooth;
transfer mixture to small bowl, stir in
remaining yogurt.
2 Serve with raw vegetable sticks and water
crackers, if you like.

white bean and garlic dip

300g can white beans,
  rinsed, drained
⅓ cup (95g) yogurt
2 tablespoons lemon juice
1 clove garlic, quartered

preparation time 5 minutes
makes 1 cup
nutritional count per ¼ cup
0.9g total fat (0.6g saturated fat);
138kJ (33 cal); 2.6g carbohydrate;
2.4g protein; 1.1g fibre

1 Blend or process ingredients until smooth.
2 Sprinkle with ground cumin and serve with raw
vegetable sticks or water crackers, if you like.

White beans is the term we use for canned navy
cannellini, haricot or great northern beans; any
of these can be used in this recipe.

tuna and cannellini bean salad

2 cups (400g) dried cannellini
  beans
425g can tuna in springwater,
  drained
1 small red onion (100g),
  sliced thinly
2 stalks celery (300g), trimmed,
  sliced thinly

preparation and cooking time
1 hour 10 minutes
(plus standing time)
serves 4
nutritional count per serving
2.5g total fat (0.9g saturated fat);
920kJ (220 cal); 16g carbohydrate;
28.5g protein; 8.2g fibre

1 Place beans in medium bowl, cover with cold water; stand overnight, drain. Rinse under cold water; drain.
2 Place beans in medium saucepan of boiling water; return to the boil. Reduce heat; simmer, uncovered, about 1 hour or until beans are almost tender. Drain.
3 Combine beans in large serving bowl with tuna, onion and celery. Dress salad with an italian dressing, if desired.

turkey on toasted turkish rolls

4 small turkish bread rolls (440g)
120g shaved cooked turkey breast
40g shaved reduced-fat
  jarlsberg cheese
40g baby spinach leaves

preparation and cooking time
10 minutes
serves 4
nutritional count per serving
7.9g total fat (2.7g saturated fat);
1522kJ (364 cal); 49.3g carbohydrate;
21.7g protein; 3.1g fibre

1 Heat sandwich press.
2 Split rolls in half. Sandwich turkey, cheese and spinach between roll halves.
3 Toast in sandwich press until browned lightly. Serve with cranberry sauce, if desired.

Any small bread rolls will do if turkish bread rolls are not available.

tip Adding avocado to this open sandwich not only adds a rich creamy flavour, it also increases its nutritional value. Avocados are a rich source of potassium and healthy monounsaturated fats that help to lower cholesterol.

tip In addition to being exquisitely tasty, prawns are also a very good health food. They're an extremely good source of protein, yet are low in fat and kilojoules. They're also a great source of omega-3 fatty acids, which help prevent against heart disease and other illnesses.

roasted cherry tomatoes, fetta and avocado on turkish bread

250g cherry tomatoes, halved

½ large loaf turkish bread (215g), halved

1 medium avocado (250g), sliced thinly

100g piece reduced-fat fetta cheese, crumbled

1 Preheat grill.

2 Cook tomato under grill about 5 minutes or until softened.

3 Meanwhile, split bread pieces horizontally; toast cut sides. Top toast with avocado, tomato and cheese; grill about 2 minutes or until hot. Serve sprinkled with basil, if desired.

preparation and cooking time
15 minutes
serves 4
nutritional count per serving
15.3g total fat (4.7g saturated fat); 1237kJ (296 cal); 25.6g carbohydrate; 12.4g protein; 3.1g fibre
Use a loaf of ciabatta bread if turkish bread is not available.

spicy prawns

1kg uncooked medium king prawns

3 cloves garlic, crushed

2 fresh long red chillies, chopped finely

2 tablespoons olive oil

1 Shell and devein prawns, leaving tails intact. Combine garlic, chilli and oil in medium bowl, add prawns; toss prawns to coat in marinade. Cover; refrigerate 3 hours or overnight.

2 Cook prawns, in batches, in heated oiled large frying pan until just changed in colour. Serve prawns with lemon wedges, if desired.

preparation and cooking time
25 minutes (plus refrigeration time)
serves 4
nutritional count per serving
9.9g total fat (1.4g saturated fat); 811kJ (194 cal); 0.3g carbohydrate; 25.8g protein; 0.4g fibre

toasted turkey baguette

2 x 10cm pieces french bread
  stick (70g), halved horizontally
150g smoked turkey breast,
  sliced thinly
1 medium green capsicum (150g),
  sliced thinly
50g shaved edam cheese

1 Preheat grill.
2 Place bread, cut-sides up, on oven tray; top each with turkey, capsicum and cheese. Heat under grill until cheese is melted.

preparation and cooking time
10 minutes
serves 4
nutritional count per serving
7.6g total fat (2.8g saturated fat);
1313kJ (314 cal); 38.1g carbohydrate;
21.4g protein; 2.9g fibre

fig and fetta crostini

125g marinated fetta cheese
1 tablespoon finely chopped
  fresh chives
24 melba toasts (50g)
3 medium fresh figs (180g)

1 Using fork, mash cheese with chives in small bowl; spread on one side of each toast.
2 Cut each fig into eight wedges; place one wedge on each toast. Sprinkle with coarsely ground black pepper, if desired.

preparation time 10 minutes
makes 24
nutritional count per crostini
1.4g total fat (0.8g saturated fat);
125kJ (30 cal); 2.8g carbohydrate;
1.4g protein; 0.3g fibre

mexican bagel

2 bagels (190g)
2 tablespoons bottled tomato salsa
1 large avocado (320g),
  sliced thinly
100g sliced cheddar cheese

1 Preheat grill.
2 Split bagels in half horizontally; spread with salsa. Top each half with avocado and cheese. Heat under grill until cheese is melted.

preparation and cooking time
10 minutes
serves 4
nutritional count per serving
14.3g total fat (5.4g saturated fat);
1053kJ (252 cal); 21g carbohydrate;
9.1g protein; 1.9g fibre

pesto chicken on pitta

⅓ cup (80g) basil pesto
4 pocket pitta bread (320g)
1 cup (160g) coarsely chopped
  barbecued chicken
1 cup (100g) coarsely grated
  pizza cheese

1 Preheat grill.
2 Spread pesto over bread; top with chicken and cheese. Heat under grill until cheese is melted.

preparation and cooking time
10 minutes
serves 4
nutritional count per serving
18.3g total fat (6.3g saturated fat);
1856kJ (444 cal); 41.8g carbohydrate;
26.4g protein; 2.7g fibre

pizza caprese

2 x 335g pizza bases with
   tomato paste
4 large egg tomatoes (360g),
   sliced thinly
210g bocconcini cheese, halved
¼ cup thinly sliced fresh basil

preparation and cooking time
25 minutes
serves 4
nutritional count per serving
14.6g total fat (6.1g saturated fat);
2658kJ (636 cal); 94.5g carbohydrate;
26.1g protein; 9g fibre

1 Preheat oven to 220°C/200°C fan-forced. Oil
two oven trays.
2 Top pizza bases with tomato and cheese. Cook,
uncovered, about 15 minutes or until cheese is
melted. Sprinkle pizzas with basil.

ham, sage and fontina pizza

2 x 335g pizza bases
200g fontina cheese, sliced thinly
2 tablespoons finely chopped
   fresh sage
100g thinly sliced ham

preparation and cooking time
20 minutes
serves 4
nutritional count per serving
22.2g total fat (10.6g saturated fat);
2934kJ (702 cal); 88.8g carbohydrate;
32.9g protein; 6.2g fibre
Instead of the fontina cheese, you
can use mozzarella, instead.

1 Preheat oven to 220°C/200°C fan-forced. Oil
two oven trays.
2 Top pizza bases with half the cheese; sprinkle
with sage then top with ham and remaining
cheese. Cook, uncovered, about 15 minutes or
until cheese is melted.

tip Commercial pizza bases are available in a full range of thicknesses. For this pizza, select a thinner base so it complements rather than competes with the flavours of the topping.

tip Fontina is a classic Italian cows-milk cheese that has been made in the Aosta Valley, in the Alps, since the 12th century. It's very rich and creamy – with a milk fat content of around 45% – and has a nutty flavour that intensifies with age. Fontina can be replaced by gruyère, edam or gouda.

pepperoni pizza

2 x 335g pizza bases with
tomato paste
125g pepperoni, sliced thinly
4 slices (170g) roasted red
capsicum, sliced thickly
1 cup (80g) flaked parmesan
cheese

preparation and cooking time
25 minutes
serves 4
nutritional count per serving
24.3g total fat (9g saturated fat);
3110kJ (744 cal); 94.7g carbohydrate;
31.8g protein; 8.1g fibre

1 Preheat oven to 220°C/200°C fan-forced. Oil two oven trays.
2 Top pizza bases with pepperoni and capsicum; sprinkle with cheese. Cook, uncovered, about 15 minutes or until cheese is melted.

spinach and beetroot tart

1 sheet ready-rolled puff pasty
250g frozen spinach,
thawed, drained
1 cup (200g) crumbled
fetta cheese
½ x 850g can drained baby
beetroot, sliced thinly

preparation and cooking time
30 minutes
serves 4
nutritional count per serving
21.4g total fat (12.8g saturated fat);
1421kJ (340 cal); 22.1g carbohydrate;
13.4g protein; 4g fibre

1 Preheat oven to 220°C/200°C fan-forced.
2 Place pastry on oiled oven tray. Fold edges of pastry over to make a 5mm border around pastry. Prick pastry base with fork. Place another oven tray on top of pastry (to stop pastry rising); bake 10 minutes. Remove top tray from pastry; reduce oven temperature to 200°C/180°C fan-forced.
3 Meanwhile, combine spinach with half the cheese in medium bowl.
4 Top tart with spinach mixture, beetroot and remaining cheese. Bake about 10 minutes.

tomato, leek and fetta tartlets

200g marinated fetta cheese
1 medium leek (350g)
2 sheets ready-rolled puff pastry
250g cherry tomatoes,
  sliced thinly

preparation and cooking time
50 minutes
makes 24
nutritional count per tartlet
5.1g total fat (1.5g saturated fat);
330kJ (79 cal); 5.6g carbohydrate;
2.5g protein; 0.6g fibre

1 Preheat oven to 220°C/200°C fan-forced.
2 Drain marinated fetta; reserve 1 tablespoon of the oil.
3 Cut leek into 6cm pieces; cut pieces in half lengthways, slice halves lengthways into thin strips. Heat reserved oil in large frying pan; cook leek, stirring occasionally, about 20 minutes or until soft.
4 Meanwhile, cut each pastry sheet into twelve 6cm x 8cm rectangles; place on lightly oiled oven trays. Fold edges of pastry over to make a 5mm border around pastry; prick pastry pieces with fork. Bake, uncovered, in oven, about 10 minutes or until browned lightly. Remove from oven; using fork, immediately press pastry pieces down to flatten. Reduce oven temperature to 200°C/180°C fan-forced.
5 Spread 1 tablespoon of the leek mixture over each pastry piece; crumble one piece of the cheese over each then top with tomato. Bake, uncovered, about 5 minutes or until tomato just softens. Serve immediately.

tip To make your own marinated fetta, cut 200g fetta cheese into 1cm pieces. Combine 2 teaspoons finely grated lemon rind, 2 tablespoons finely chopped fresh oregano and 1 cup chilli-infused olive oil in small jug. Place cheese in sterilised jar; pour over oil mixture. Refrigerate 3 hours or overnight. Store any unused marinated fetta in the refrigerator.

35

chicken tikka drumettes

12 chicken drumettes (960g)
⅓ cup (100g) tikka masala paste
½ cup (140g) yogurt
¼ cup coarsely chopped
    fresh coriander

preparation and cooking time
30 minutes
serves 4
nutritional count per serving
21.7g total fat (5.3g saturated fat);
1346kJ (322 cal); 3.6g carbohydrate;
27.3g protein; 2.6g fibre
Substitute chicken wings for the
drumettes, if you like.

1 Preheat oven to 200°C/180°C fan-forced.
2 Place chicken in large bowl with combined paste and 2 tablespoons of the yogurt; toss to coat chicken in paste mixture. Place chicken, in single layer, on wire rack in large baking dish. Roast, uncovered, about 20 minutes or until chicken is browned and cooked through.
3 Combine coriander and remaining yogurt in small bowl. Serve chicken with yogurt mixture.

chicken and avocado quesadillas

8 large flour tortillas (470g)
125g spreadable cream cheese
2 cups (320g) shredded
    barbecued chicken
1 large avocado (320g), mashed

Serve quesadillas cut into quarters.
preparation and cooking time
20 minutes
serves 4
nutritional count per serving
38.8g total fat (12.9g saturated fat);
2579kJ (617 cal); 36.3g carbohydrate;
29.6g protein; 3.2g fibre

1 Preheat sandwich press.
2 Spread four tortillas with cream cheese then top with chicken.
3 Spread remaining tortillas with avocado; place, avocado-side down, on chicken tortillas.
4 Toast in sandwich press until golden brown.

cheese-filled zucchini flowers

200g green peppercorn cream
cheese, softened
¼ cup (15g) fresh breadcrumbs
16 baby zucchini with flowers
attached (320g)
2 tablespoons olive oil

preparation and cooking time
30 minutes
serves 4
nutritional count per serving
26g total fat (11.9g saturated fat);
1162kJ (278 cal); 5.3g carbohydrate;
5.7g protein; 1.4g fibre

1 Combine cheese and breadcrumbs in small
bowl. Discard stamens from zucchini flowers;
fill flowers with cheese mixture, twist petal
tops to enclose filling.
2 Meanwhile, heat oil in large frying pan; cook
zucchini, covered, turning occasionally and
gently, about 5 minutes or until zucchini are
tender. Serve immediately.

zucchini and sumac fritters

6 medium zucchini (700g),
grated coarsely
1¼ cups (85g) stale breadcrumbs
3 eggs
1 teaspoon sumac

preparation and cooking time
25 minutes
serves 4
nutritional count per serving
5.2g total fat (1.4g saturated fat);
677kJ (162 cal); 16.9g carbohydrate;
10g protein; 3.7g fibre

1 Squeeze excess liquid from zucchini using
absorbent paper until as dry as possible.
Combine zucchini in medium bowl with
breadcrumbs, eggs and sumac.
2 Cook tablespoons of zucchini mixture in oiled
large frying pan, in batches, until browned both
sides and cooked through. Serve with thick
greek-style yogurt, if you like.

Lunchbox

Forget that same old sandwich you have every day. Be inspired to liven up your lunchbox and avoid the humdrum with these flavour-packed rolls, salads, sandwiches and wraps.

lamb, tabbouleh and hummus on pitta

4 pocket pittas (340g),
  split lengthways
⅓ cup (65g) hummus
1 cup tabbouleh (185g)
200g thinly sliced roast lamb

1 Spread pitta with hummus; sandwich with tabbouleh and lamb. Cut in half to serve.

preparation time 5 minutes
serves 4
nutritional count per serving
18.1g total fat (5g saturated fat);
1998kJ (478 cal); 49.4g carbohydrate;
25.8g protein; 6.9g fibre

smoked trout salad roll

200g flaked smoked trout
¼ cup (60g) light sour cream
1 tablespoon finely chopped
  fresh dill
4 wholemeal bread rolls (400g),
  split in half

1 Combine trout, sour cream and dill in small bowl. Sandwich rolls with filling.

preparation time 10 minutes
serves 4
nutritional count per serving
11.3g total fat (4.9g saturated fat);
1459kJ (349 cal); 37.8g carbohydrate;
21.1g protein; 4.8g fibre

tip Hummus is a dip made from chickpeas. In fact, hummus is the Arabic word for chickpea. It has been around for thousands of years and is eaten throughout the Middle East, the Mediterranean and in many parts of India (which is why it is spelled in myriad ways – hoummos, hommos, hommus, homous), and is now popular around the world. Hummus is often eaten with pita bread or vegetables, and can be used a substitute for butter on a sandwich.

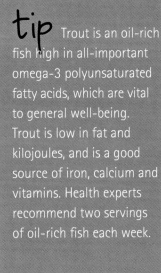

tip Trout is an oil-rich fish high in all-important omega-3 polyunsaturated fatty acids, which are vital to general well-being. Trout is low in fat and kilojoules, and is a good source of iron, calcium and vitamins. Health experts recommend two servings of oil-rich fish each week.

Each sandwich filling, on these two pages, makes one sandwich. Use any type of bread or roll you like.

egg, tomato and mayonnaise filling

1 small tomato (100g), chopped finely
1 tablespoon coarsely grated cheddar cheese
1 hard-boiled egg, chopped finely
1 tablespoon mayonnaise

1 Combine ingredients in small bowl.

preparation time 5 minutes
serves 1
nutritional count per serving
16.8g total fat (5.8g saturated fat);
932kJ (223 cal); 5.7g carbohydrate;
12.1g protein; 1.3g fibre

tuna and sweet corn filling

½ x 185g can tuna in springwater, drained
2 tablespoons canned sweet corn kernels, rinsed, drained
1 tablespoon mayonnaise

1 Combine ingredients in small bowl.

preparation time 5 minutes
serves 1
nutritional count per serving
8.2g total fat (1.5g saturated fat);
790kJ (189 cal); 8.7g carbohydrate;
19.6g protein; 1g fibre

cheese, sausage and pickle filling

1 tablespoon sweet mustard pickle
1 slice cheddar cheese
1 cold cooked beef sausage,
   sliced thickly

1 Sandwich ingredients between bread slices or roll halves.

preparation time 5 minutes
serves 1
nutritional count per serving
17.3g total fat (9.3g saturated fat);
1028kJ (246 cal); 6.8g carbohydrate;
15.3g protein; 1.7g fibre

chicken, avocado and cream cheese filling

¼ cup (40g) coarsely chopped
   barbecued chicken
¼ small avocado (50g),
   coarsely chopped
1 tablespoon spreadable
   cream cheese
¼ cup loosely packed
   mixed salad leaves

1 Combine chicken and avocado in small bowl. Spread cream cheese on bread or roll; sandwich with chicken mixture and salad leaves.

preparation time 5 minutes
serves 1
nutritional count per serving
19.5g total fat (7.1g saturated fat);
882kJ (211 cal); 0.7g carbohydrate;
8.2g protein; 0.8g fibre

salmon and cucumber bagel

400g can red salmon, drained
1 lebanese cucumber (130g),
  chopped finely
¼ cup spreadable cream cheese
2 bagels (190g)

1 Discard skin and bones from salmon. Combine salmon in small bowl with cucumber and cheese.
2 Split bagels in half; spread salmon mixture over bagels.

preparation time 10 minutes
serves 4
nutritional count per serving
16.6g total fat (6.7g saturated fat);
1467kJ (351 cal); 24.6g carbohydrate;
24.8g protein; 1.8g fibre
Pack salmon mixture in a separate container in lunchbox, and spread over bagels at lunchtime.

roast beef and slaw pockets

4 pocket pitta bread (340g)
200g coleslaw
¼ cup coarsely chopped fresh
  flat-leaf parsley leaves
200g thinly sliced roast beef

1 Split pitta bread a little more than halfway through. Combine coleslaw and parsley in small bowl.
2 Fill pockets with slaw mixture and roast beef.

preparation time 10 minutes
serves 4
nutritional count per serving
10g total fat (3.2g saturated fat);
1689kJ (404 cal); 50.8g carbohydrate;
25g protein; 3.9g fibre

prosciutto, blue brie and fig finger sandwiches

50g blue brie cheese, softened
8 slices light rye bread
6 slices prosciutto (90g),
   halved crossways
4 medium figs (240g),
   sliced thinly

1 Spread cheese over four bread slices; top with prosciutto, fig and remaining bread.
2 Remove and discard crusts; cut sandwiches into three fingers.

preparation time 10 minutes
makes 12
nutritional count per finger
2.5g total fat (1.1g saturated fat);
368kJ (88 cal); 12g carbohydrate;
4.5g protein; 1.9g fibre

chicken, capers and mayonnaise finger sandwiches

2 cups (320g) coarsely shredded
   barbecued chicken
2 tablespoons rinsed, drained
   capers, chopped coarsely
⅓ cup (100g) mayonnaise
8 slices brown bread

1 Combine chicken, capers and ¼ cup of the mayonnaise in medium bowl.
2 Spread chicken mixture over four bread slices. Spread remaining mayonnaise over remaining bread slices; place on top of chicken mixture.
3 Remove and discard crusts; cut sandwiches into three fingers.

preparation time 10 minutes
makes 12
nutritional count per finger
4.3g total fat (0.7g saturated fat);
426kJ (102 cal); 9.6g carbohydrate;
5.6g protein; 1g fibre

Creating rice paper rolls (or summer rolls) can be a fun group meal. Simply place the ingredients (rice sheets and fillings) on the table and let everyone construct their own rolls. Rice paper is a magical ingredient to work with, turning from a brittle sheet when dry into a malleable and strong wrapping when wet.

Rice paper rolls are a central part of Vietnamese cuisine. They traditionally contain pork, shrimp, herbs and rice vermicelli and are regarded as perfect snack food. They are served cold or at room temperature, accompanied by any number of dipping sauces.

hoisin and **chicken** rice paper rolls

12 x 17cm-square rice paper
sheets
2 tablespoons hoisin sauce
1¼ cups (200g) finely shredded
barbecued chicken
50g snow peas, trimmed,
sliced thinly

preparation time 25 minutes
makes 12
nutritional count per roll
1.1g total fat (0.3g saturated fat);
156kJ (42 cal); 4.6g carbohydrate;
3.1g protein; 0.6g fibre

1 Place one sheet of rice paper in medium bowl of warm water until just softened; lift sheet carefully from water, place on a tea-towel covered board with a corner point facing towards you. Place a little of the sauce and chicken vertically down centre of rice paper; top with snow peas.
2 Fold corner point facing you up over filling; roll rice paper sheet over to enclose filling. Repeat with remaining rice paper sheets and ingredients.

To keep rice paper rolls moist in the lunchbox, wrap a in moist paper towel, then in plastic wrap.

smoked **salmon** and avocado rice paper rolls

12 x 17cm-square rice paper
sheets
½ medium avocado (125g),
sliced thinly
100g thinly sliced smoked
salmon, cut into strips
½ cup firmly packed fresh
coriander leaves

preparation time 25 minutes
makes 12
nutritional count per roll
2.2g total fat (0.5g saturated fat);
184kJ (44 cal); 3.2g carbohydrate;
2.7g protein; 0.3g fibre

1 Place one sheet of rice paper in medium bowl of warm water until just softened; lift sheet carefully from water, place on a tea-towel covered board with a corner point facing towards you. Place one slice avocado vertically down centre of rice paper, top with salmon and coriander.
2 Fold top and bottom corner points over filling; roll rice paper sheet over to enclose filling. Repeat with remaining rice paper sheets and ingredients.

To keep rice paper rolls moist in the lunchbox, wrap in a moist paper towel, then in plastic wrap.

olive, cream cheese and rocket wraps

100g spreadable cream cheese
¼ cup coarsely chopped seeded
  kalamata olives
4 slices mountain bread (100g)
20g baby rocket leaves

1 Combine cream cheese and olives in small bowl.
2 Spread cheese mixture evenly over bread, leaving a 3cm border; top each with rocket. Roll up bread to enclose filling; cut in half to serve, if you like.

preparation time 10 minutes
serves 4
nutritional count per wrap
8.7g total fat (5.4g saturated fat);
669kJ (160 cal); 15g carbohydrate;
5g protein; 1.4g fibre

mortadella, mozzarella and roast capsicum roll

4 white bread rolls (200g), halved
100g thinly sliced
  mozzarella cheese
4 slices mortadella (80g)
100g drained thinly sliced
  char-grilled capsicum

1 Sandwich bread rolls with cheese, mortadella, and capsicum.

preparation time 10 minutes
serves 4
nutritional count per roll
12.2g total fat (5g saturated fat);
986kJ (236 cal); 19g carbohydrate;
11.7g protein; 1.5g fibre

roast beef and horseradish cream on focaccia

2 tablespoons horseradish cream
4 focaccia rolls (440g), halved
200g thinly sliced roast beef
50g baby rocket leaves

1 Spread horseradish cream on four roll halves; top with beef, rocket and remaining rolls.

preparation time 5 minutes
serves 4
nutritional count per serving
7.1g total fat (2.3g saturated fat);
1547kJ (370 cal); 50.9g carbohydrate;
23.2g protein; 3.2g fibre

pea, ricotta and mint lavash pinwheels

½ cup (60g) frozen peas
150g low-fat ricotta cheese
1 tablespoon finely chopped
  fresh mint
4 slices lavash (240g)

1 Boil, steam or microwave peas until tender; drain, cool. Using fork, lightly crush peas. Combine pea mash with cheese and mint.
2 Spread pea mixture over bread, leaving 3cm border. Roll bread to enclose filling. Slice rolls thickly.

preparation and cooking time
15 minutes
serves 4
nutritional count per serving
5.6g total fat (2.9g saturated fat);
1062kJ (254 cal); 37.9g carbohydrate;
10.9g protein; 3g fibre

tuna salad

125g can flavoured sliced tuna
  in oil, drained
25g baby spinach leaves
6 cherry tomatoes, halved
2 tablespoons bottled
  french dressing

1 Combine ingredients in medium bowl.

preparation time 5 minutes
serves 1
nutritional count per serving
14.9g total fat (2.2g saturated fat);
978kJ (234 cal); 4.6g carbohydrate;
21.2g protein; 1.6g fibre
Use flavoured tuna such as chilli
and herbs or lemon and garlic.

lentil, beetroot and rocket salad

½ cup rinsed, drained canned
  brown lentils
½ cup drained canned
  baby beetroot halves
25g baby rocket leaves
2 tablespoons bottled
  balsamic dressing

1 Combine ingredients in medium bowl.

preparation time 5 minutes
serves 1
nutritional count per serving
1.1g total fat (0.1g saturated fat);
577kJ (138 cal); 18.7g carbohydrate;
9.7g protein; 6.9g fibre

deli pasta salad

375g large spiral pasta
250g mixed antipasto vegetables, drained
100g sliced salami, cut into strips
¼ cup (60ml) bottled italian dressing

1 Cook pasta in large saucepan of boiling water, uncovered, until tender. Drain pasta, rinse under cold water.

2 Combine pasta with vegetables, salami and dressing in large bowl.

preparation and cooking time
20 minutes
serves 4
nutritional count per serving
15.8g total fat (4g saturated fat); 2077kJ (497 cal); 69g carbohydrate; 17.7g protein; 2.5g fibre

tip We used grilled eggplant, capsicum and sun-dried tomatoes for the antipasto vegetables. Grilled artichokes and mushrooms could also be used.

34

Mid-week Meals

Let's face it, the week is busy and we don't have time for fiddly and time-consuming dinners. But you wouldn't know it with these impressive yet easy meals – they're on the table in a flash.

beef sirloin with herb butter

60g butter, softened
1 clove garlic
¼ cup finely chopped fresh
   mixed herbs
4 x 250g beef sirloin steaks

preparation and cooking time
30 minutes (plus refrigeration time)
serves 4
nutritional count per serving
35.1g total fat (18.4g saturated fat);
2186kJ (523 cal); 0.2g carbohydrate;
52.1g protein; 0.2g fibre

1 Place butter, garlic and herbs in small bowl; stir until combined. Place on piece of plastic wrap, shape into a rectangular block; wrap tightly, refrigerate until firm.
2 Cook beef in heated oiled large frying pan until browned both sides and cooked as desired. Cover; stand 5 minutes. Top steaks with butter. Serve with thin chips, if you like.

fillet steak, cheese and capsicum stacks

1 medium red capsicum (200g)
4 beef fillet steaks (500g)
4 thick slices gouda cheese (125g)
20g baby spinach leaves

preparation and cooking time
25 minutes
serves 4
nutritional count per serving
17.2g total fat (9.3g saturated fat);
1271kJ (304 cal); 1.7g carbohydrate;
35.3g protein; 0.6g fibre

1 Quarter capsicum; remove seeds and membranes. Roast capsicum under hot grill, skin-side up, until skin blisters and blackens. Cover with plastic or paper for 5 minutes then peel away skin.
2 Preheat oven to 220°C/200°C fan-forced.
3 Cut steaks in half horizontally; divide cheese, spinach and capsicum among four steak halves, top with remaining steaks. Tie stacks with kitchen string; cook, uncovered, in heated oiled large frying pan until browned both sides. Transfer to oven tray; cook, uncovered, in oven about 10 minutes or until cooked as desired.
4 If you like, serve stacks with mashed potatoes and peas.

tip Use herbs such as parsley, basil and chives. Sirloin is a full-flavoured steak and is considered one of the cheaper of the premium steaks. Instead of the sirloin you could use rib eye, rump or eye fillet steak.

tip Also known as filet mignon, tenderloin, tournedos, chateaubriand and beef medallions, fillet steak is considered by most chefs as the best steak because it's the most tender cut of beef. It's also the most expensive cut of steak, but has very little fat and is fast cooking.

herb-crumbed beef fillets

Use fresh herbs such as basil, chives and rosemary.

4 x 200g beef scotch fillet steak
1¼ cups fresh breadcrumbs
40g butter, melted
2 tablespoons finely chopped
    fresh mixed herbs

preparation and cooking time
30 minutes
serves 4
nutritional count per serving
20.9g total fat (10.5g saturated fat);
1760kJ (421 cal); 12.9g carbohydrate;
44.9g protein; 0.9g fibre

1 Cook steaks, uncovered, in heated oiled large frying pan until cooked as desired; place on oven tray.
2 Meanwhile, combine breadcrumbs, butter and herbs in small bowl.
3 Preheat grill. Sprinkle breadcrumb mixture over top of steaks; brown lightly under grill.

veal with basil mayo

4 x 170g veal cutlets
2 cups fresh basil leaves
4 slices prosciutto (60g)
½ cup (150g) mayonnaise

preparation and cooking time
30 minutes
serves 4
nutritional count per serving
9.7g total fat (1.9g saturated fat);
986kJ (236 cal); 3.3g carbohydrate;
33.3g protein; 0.6g fibre

1 Preheat oven to 200°C/180°C fan-forced.
2 Oil two oven trays. Place cutlets on one tray; top each with 3 basil leaves and a prosciutto slice (secure to cutlet with toothpick if necessary). Roast, uncovered, 20 minutes or until cutlets are cooked as desired.
3 Chop remaining basil finely; mix with mayonnaise in small bowl.
4 Serve cutlets topped with basil mayonnaise.

bacon-wrapped steaks with tarragon butter

60g butter, softened
2 teaspoons finely chopped
  fresh tarragon
4 rindless bacon rashers (260g)
4 x 150g beef fillet steaks

preparation and cooking time
30 minutes (plus refrigeration time)
serves 4
nutritional count per serving
24.9g total fat (13.2g saturated fat);
1697kJ (406 cal); 0.4g carbohydrate;
45.6g protein; 0g fibre

1 Combine butter and tarragon in small bowl. Place on piece of plastic wrap; shape into 6cm log, wrap tightly. Refrigerate until firm.
2 Wrap bacon around steaks; secure with toothpicks. Cook steaks, uncovered, in heated oiled large frying pan, until cooked as desired. Cover steaks; stand 5 minutes.
3 Serve steaks topped with butter.

steak with mustard cream

1kg piece beef eye fillet, cut into
  four steaks
3/4 cup (180ml) dry white wine
250g crème fraîche
1 tablespoon wholegrain mustard

preparation and cooking time
30 minutes
serves 4
nutritional count per serving
39.9g total fat (22.6g saturated fat);
2558kJ (612 cal); 2.1g carbohydrate;
54.4g protein; 0.1g fibre

1 Heat oiled large frying pan; cook steaks, in batches, until browned both sides and cooked as desired. Cover to keep warm.
2 Place wine in same frying pan; bring to the boil, stirring. Reduce heat; simmer, uncovered, 1 minute. Whisk in crème fraîche and mustard; simmer, uncovered, about 2 minutes or until sauce thickens slightly.
3 Drizzle steaks with the sauce; serve with chips, if you like.

veal campagnola

4 large veal steaks (500g)
2 cups (500ml) bottled tomato
  pasta sauce
3 cups (200g) thawed, drained
  frozen spinach
2 cups (200g) coarsely grated
  mozzarella cheese

preparation and cooking time
25 minutes
serves 4
nutritional count per serving
14.5g total fat (7.9g saturated fat);
1852kJ (443 cal); 32g carbohydrate;
42.9g protein; 5.6g fibre

1 Place veal between two pieces of plastic wrap; pound until each piece is of the same thickness. Discard plastic wrap.
2 Cook veal in heated oiled large frying pan until browned both sides; drain on absorbent paper.
3 Add pasta sauce to same pan; bring to the boil. Place veal, in single layer, on top of boiling sauce. Spread a quarter of the spinach on top of each piece of veal then top with cheese. Cover; let mixture simmer about 1 minute or until cheese melts.

veal with capers and lemon

8 veal steaks (800g)
¼ cup (60ml) lemon juice
½ cup (125ml) beef stock
¼ cup (50g) rinsed, drained,
  capers, coarsely chopped

preparation and cooking time
20 minutes
serves 4
nutritional count per serving
3.1g total fat (0.8g saturated fat);
911kJ (218 cal); 1.6g carbohydrate;
45.1g protein; 0.2g fibre

1 Cook veal in heated oiled large frying pan, in batches, until browned both sides and cooked as desired. Remove from pan; cover to keep warm.
2 Add juice and stock to pan; bring to the boil. Reduce heat; simmer, uncovered, 1 minute. Stir in capers. Serve sliced veal with sauce; sprinkle with parsley leaves, if desired.

peppered veal medallions

8 veal medallions (640g)
2 tablespoons drained, canned
   green peppercorns,
   chopped finely
½ cup (125ml) brandy
⅓ cup (80g) sour cream

preparation and cooking time
35 minutes
serves 4
nutritional count per serving
10.3g total fat (5.9g saturated fat);
1296kJ (310 cal); 1.9g carbohydrate;
36.2g protein; 0g fibre

1 Combine veal, peppercorns and brandy in medium bowl, cover; stand 10 minutes. Drain veal; reserve marinade.
2 Cook veal in heated oiled large frying pan until browned both sides and cooked as desired. Remove from pan; cover to keep warm.
3 Add reserved marinade to pan; bring to the boil. Remove from heat; stir in sour cream. Return to heat; simmer about 5 minutes or until sauce thickens.
4 Spoon sauce over veal; accompany with steamed beans and potatoes, if desired.

tarragon chicken skewers

4 chicken breast fillets (800g),
   sliced thickly
1 tablespoon finely chopped
   fresh tarragon
1 tablespoon wholegrain mustard

preparation and cooking time
25 minutes (plus refrigeration time)
serves 4
nutritional count per serving
9.4g total fat (2.9g saturated fat);
974kJ (233 cal); 0.2g carbohydrate;
36.6g protein; 0.2g fibre

1 Thread equal amounts of chicken onto each of 12 skewers. Using fingers, press combined tarragon and mustard all over chicken, cover skewers; refrigerate 30 minutes.
2 Cook skewers in heated oiled large frying pan until browned lightly and cooked though.

Soak bamboo skewers in cold water for at least an hour before using to prevent them from splintering and scorching during cooking.

tip Saltimbocca is a Roman specialty (the word means "jumps in the mouth"); it's made from very thin slices of meat, usually veal, topped with sage leaves and prosciutto or ham, rolled and sautéed in butter and wine.

tip Basil is one of the easiest and most useful herbs to grow. You don't need a large kitchen garden: a pot or a window box in a protected, sunny position is sufficient. Basil will grow year-round (depending on the climate) and you can freeze the leaves for later use.

veal saltimbocca

4 x 100g veal schnitzels
4 fresh sage leaves
4 rindless middle bacon strips
  (260g)
1 cup (250ml) dry white wine

preparation and cooking time
20 minutes
serves 4
nutritional count per serving
10.1g total fat (3.6g saturated fat);
1145kJ (274 cal); 0.4g carbohydrate;
35g protein; 0g fibre

1 Roll each schnitzel, top with sage leaves. Wrap one bacon strip around each schnitzel; secure with toothpicks or small skewers.
2 Cook schnitzel in heated oiled large frying pan, bacon seam-side down, turning occasionally, until cooked. Remove from pan.
3 Pour wine into pan; bring to the boil, stirring. Boil until liquid is reduced by half. Drizzle saltimbocca with sauce; serve with chips, if you like.

chicken with roasted cherry tomato and basil sauce

500g cherry tomatoes
4 chicken breast fillets (800g)
¼ cup coarsely chopped
  fresh basil
¼ cup (60ml) cream

preparation and cooking time
35 minutes
serves 4
nutritional count per serving
17.6g total fat (7.9g saturated fat);
1463kJ (350 cal); 3.2g carbohydrate;
43.7g protein; 2.1g fibre

1 Preheat oven to 200°C/180°C fan-forced.
2 Place tomatoes in large shallow baking dish; spray with cooking-oil spray. Roast, uncovered, about 20 minutes or until tomatoes soften.
3 Meanwhile, cook chicken in heated oiled large frying pan until cooked through. Cover; stand 5 minutes.
4 Blend or process half the tomatoes until smooth. Place in medium saucepan with basil and cream; cook, stirring, over low heat, until heated through. Serve chicken topped with sauce and remaining tomatoes.

rosemary, brie and sun-dried tomato chicken

30g sun-dried tomatoes, chopped finely
1 tablespoon finely chopped fresh rosemary
4 chicken breast fillets (800g)
60g firm brie cheese, quartered

preparation and cooking time
30 minutes

serves 4

nutritional count per serving
19.6g total fat (6.4g saturated fat);
2048kJ (490 cal); 25.6g carbohydrate;
47.4g protein; 10.7g fibre

1 Combine tomato and rosemary in small bowl.
2 Using small sharp knife, slit a pocket in one side of each breast fillet, taking care not to cut all the way through. Divide tomato mixture and cheese among pockets; secure openings with toothpicks.
3 Cook chicken in heated oiled large frying pan until browned both sides and cooked through. Serve with mashed potato, if desired.

pan-fried chicken with chilli butter

60g butter, softened
½ teaspoon dried chilli flakes
1 tablespoon coarsely chopped drained semi-dried tomatoes in oil
4 chicken thigh fillets (800g)

preparation and cooking time
25 minutes (plus refrigeration time)
serves 4

nutritional count per serving
26.9g total fat (12.5g saturated fat);
1647kJ (394 cal); 1g carbohydrate;
37.6g protein; 0.4g fibre

1 Combine butter, chilli and tomatoes in small bowl. Place mixture on piece of plastic wrap, shape into rectangular block, wrap tightly; place in refrigerator until firm.
2 Meanwhile, cook chicken in heated oiled large frying pan until browned both sides and cooked through. Serve chicken with butter slices, and roasted potato wedges, if desired.

maple-glazed chicken, shallot and kumara skewers

1 large kumara (500g), cut into
  2cm pieces
660g chicken thigh fillets, cut
  into 3cm pieces
12 shallots (300g), halved
2 tablespoons pure maple syrup

preparation and cooking time
40 minutes
makes 8
nutritional count per skewer
6.1g total fat (1.8g saturated fat);
736kJ (176 cal); 12.9g carbohydrate;
16.8g protein; 1.3g fibre

1 Boil, steam or microwave kumara until just tender; drain. Thread kumara, chicken and shallot, alternately, onto skewers.
2 Cook skewers in heated oiled large frying pan, covered with foil, 10 minutes. Uncover, brush skewers all over with syrup. Turn; cook, brushing occasionally with syrup, about 5 minutes or until chicken is cooked through.

You need eight bamboo skewers for this recipe. Soak them in cold water for at least an hour before using to prevent them from splintering and scorching during cooking.

mexican-style chicken

4 chicken breast fillets (800g)
35g packet taco seasoning mix
1 fresh small red thai chilli,
  finely chopped
1 tablespoon lime juice

preparation and cooking time
25 minutes
serves 4
nutritional count per serving
11g total fat (3.5g saturated fat);
1225kJ (293 cal); 3.6g carbohydrate;
43.3g protein; 0.9g fibre

1 Combine ingredients in medium bowl; refrigerate 10 minutes.
2 Cook chicken in heated oiled large frying pan until browned both sides and cooked through. Serve with grilled corn, if desired.

roast lemon and cumin chicken

2 medium lemons (280g)
2 tablespoons olive oil
1½ tablespoons ground cumin
2kg whole chicken

preparation and cooking time
1 hour 35 minutes
(plus standing time)
serves 4
nutritional count per serving
41.7g total fat (11.5g saturated fat);
2470kJ (591 cal); 1.3g carbohydrate;
52.6g protein; 1.8g fibre

1 Preheat oven to 200°C/180°C fan-forced.
2 Juice one lemon (you need 2 tablespoons); cut remaining lemon into wedges.
3 Combine oil, cumin and juice in small bowl. Place lemon wedges in cavity of chicken. Rub skin all over with cumin mixture; tie chicken legs together with kitchen string.
4 Half fill large baking dish with water; place chicken on oiled wire rack over dish. Roast 20 minutes. Reduce oven temperature to 180°C/160°C fan-forced; roast chicken about 1 hour or until cooked. Remove chicken from rack; cover, stand 20 minutes before serving.

chicken with prosciutto and capers

4 slices prosciutto (60g)
4 chicken breast fillets (800g)
60g butter
2 tablespoons rinsed, drained
  baby capers

preparation and cooking time
25 minutes
serves 4
nutritional count per serving
24.2g total fat (11.8g saturated fat);
1685kJ (403 cal); 0.8g carbohydrate;
45.7g protein; 0.1g fibre

1 Wrap one slice of prosciutto tightly around each breast fillet.
2 Cook chicken in heated oiled large frying pan until cooked through; remove from pan, cover to keep warm.
3 Melt butter in same pan, add capers; cook, stirring, about 2 minutes or until crisp.
4 Serve chicken with caper sauce, and lemon wedges, if desired.

dukkah-crumbed chicken

2 eggs
1/4 cup (25g) dukkah spice mixture
1/2 cup (50g) packaged
  breadcrumbs
8 chicken thigh fillets (1.5kg)

preparation and cooking time
30 minutes
serves 4
nutritional count per serving
24.4g total fat (6.8g saturated fat);
1948kJ (466 cal); 8.6g carbohydrate;
52.8g protein; 1.1g fibre
Dukkah is a traditional Egyptian mix
of various roasted nuts, seeds and
spices. It is available from spice shops.

1 Lightly beat eggs in medium shallow bowl.
Combine dukkah and breadcrumbs in another
medium shallow bowl.
2 Coat chicken, all over, in beaten egg then coat
with dukkah mixture.
3 Cook chicken in heated oiled large frying pan
until browned both sides and cooked through.

cashew crumbed pork schnitzel

4 pork medallions (600g)
1 cup (150g) roasted
  unsalted cashews
1/2 cup (35g) stale breadcrumbs
1 egg

preparation and cooking time
35 minutes
serves 4
nutritional count per serving
24.3g total fat (5g saturated fat);
1852kJ (443 cal); 12.3g carbohydrate;
42.7g protein; 2.6g fibre

1 Place pork between two pieces of plastic wrap;
pound each piece until about 5mm thick.
2 Blend or process nuts until coarsely chopped;
combine in medium shallow bowl with
breadcrumbs. Whisk egg lightly in another
medium shallow bowl. Dip pork in egg then
coat in cashew mixture.
3 Cook pork in heated oiled large frying pan until
cooked as desired. Drain on absorbent paper.

creamy garlic and herb chicken

4 chicken breast fillets (800g)
3 cloves garlic, crushed
300ml cream
2 tablespoons coarsely chopped
 fresh oregano

preparation and cooking time
25 minutes
serves 4
nutritional count per serving
15.3g total fat (8.9g saturated fat);
857kJ (205 cal); 0.8g carbohydrate;
15.8g protein; 0.2g fibre

1 Cook chicken in heated oiled large frying pan about 15 minutes or until cooked through. Remove from pan; cover to keep warm.
2 Cook garlic in same pan, stirring, 1 minute. Add cream; bring to the boil. Reduce heat; simmer, uncovered, about 5 minutes or until mixture thickens slightly. Stir in oregano.
3 Drizzle sauce over chicken; serve with boiled gnocchi, if desired.

roasted pork fillet with apricot relish

800g can apricot halves in syrup
600g pork fillets
2 tablespoons white vinegar
¼ cup (40g) sultanas

preparation and cooking time
30 minutes
serves 4
nutritional count per serving
3.5g total fat (1.2g saturated fat);
1070kJ (256 cal); 19.2g carbohydrate;
34.6g protein; 3.4g fibre

1 Preheat oven to 240°C/220°C fan-forced.
2 Drain apricots over small bowl. Reserve half the juice; chop apricots coarsely.
3 Place pork in oiled baking dish; spray with cooking-oil spray. Roast, uncovered, about 20 minutes or until pork is cooked as desired. Cover; stand 5 minutes then slice thickly.
4 Meanwhile, combine apricot, reserved juice, vinegar, sultanas and ½ cup water in medium saucepan; bring to the boil. Reduce heat; simmer, uncovered, about 20 minutes or until relish thickens slightly. Serve pork with relish and steamed snow peas, if you like.

tip Gnocchi (Italian dumplings) are traditionally eaten as an entree alternative to soup and pasta and are most commonly made from potato or semolina. They are available dried, frozen and fresh – in refrigerated vacuum-sealed packs – from supermarkets and Italian grocery stores.

tip The leanest cuts of pork come from the pork loin, fillet (or tenderloin) and the leg, trimmed of fat. You can always ask your butcher to trim the meat. Pork can dry out if overcooked and is most succulent when cooked with a hint of pink in the middle.

pork with maple mustard sauce

4 pork midloin butterfly steaks
(800g)
2 tablespoons wholegrain mustard
¼ cup (60ml) pure maple syrup
½ cup (125ml) dry white wine

preparation and cooking time
30 minutes
serves 4
nutritional count per serving
20.6g total fat (6.8g saturated fat);
1814kJ (434 cal); 13.8g carbohydrate;
43.2g protein; 0.2g fibre

1 Place pork in shallow dish, pour over combined mustard and syrup; stand 10 minutes. Drain pork; reserve marinade.
2 Cook pork in heated oiled large frying pan until cooked as desired. Remove pork from pan; cover to keep warm.
3 Combine reserved marinade and wine in same pan; bring to the boil. Reduce heat; simmer, uncovered, until sauce is thickened slightly. Drizzle sauce over pork; sprinkle with chopped parsley, if desired.

honey soy pork cutlets

¼ cup (60ml) light soy sauce
2 tablespoons honey
2 cloves garlic, crushed
4 pork cutlets (720g)

preparation and cooking time
25 minutes (plus refrigeration time)
serves 4
nutritional count per serving
12.1g total fat (4.1g saturated fat);
1024kJ (245 cal); 12.3g carbohydrate;
21.5g protein; 0.3g fibre

1 Combine ingredients in large bowl. Cover; refrigerate 3 hours or overnight.
2 Cook drained pork in heated oiled large frying pan until cooked as desired. Serve with steamed asian vegetables, if you like.

pork medallions with capsicum cream sauce

1 medium red capsicum (200g)
2 cloves garlic, crushed
4 pork medallions (600g)
½ cup (125ml) cream

preparation and cooking time
25 minutes
serves 4
nutritional count per serving
28.9g total fat (14g saturated fat);
1689kJ (404 cal); 2.7g carbohydrate;
33.5g protein; 0.7g fibre

1 Quarter capsicum; discard seeds and membranes. Roast capsicum under grill or in very hot oven, skin-side up, until skin blisters and blackens. Cover capsicum with plastic or paper for 5 minutes; peel away skin then slice capsicum thickly.
2 Cook garlic in heated oiled large frying pan until fragrant. Add capsicum and ½ cup water; cook, uncovered, 5 minutes.
3 Meanwhile, cook pork in heated oiled large frying pan until cooked as desired. Cover to keep warm.
4 Blend or process capsicum mixture until smooth. Return to same pan, add cream; bring to the boil. Reduce heat; simmer, uncovered, 5 minutes. Serve pork drizzled with sauce.

pan-fried pork fillets with pear balsamic sauce

600g pork fillets
1 cup (250ml) pear juice
1 tablespoon balsamic vinegar
1 fresh long red chilli,
    chopped finely

preparation and cooking time
20 minutes
serves 4
nutritional count per serving
3.5g total fat (1.2g saturated fat);
798kJ (191 cal); 6.2g carbohydrate;
33.1g protein; 0g fibre

1 Cook pork in heated oiled large frying pan until cooked as desired. Cover; stand 5 minutes.
2 Meanwhile, add remaining ingredients to same pan; bring to the boil. Reduce heat; simmer about 5 minutes or until liquid reduces by half. Serve sliced pork drizzled with sauce.

tamarind and **date** pork braise

600g pork fillets, sliced thinly
1 fresh long red chilli,
   chopped finely
2 shallots (50g), sliced thinly
½ cup tamarind and date chutney

preparation and cooking time
25 minutes
serves 4
nutritional count per serving
3.6g total fat (1.2g saturated fat);
995kJ (238 cal); 17.2g carbohydrate;
33.2g protein; 1g fibre

1 Cook pork, in batches, in heated oiled large frying pan until browned.
2 Add chilli and shallot to same pan; cook, stirring, until shallot is soft.
3 Return pork to the pan with chutney and ⅓ cup water; bring to the boil. Reduce heat; simmer, covered, about 5 minutes or until pork is cooked as desired.

Tamarind and date chutney is available from some delicatessens and specialty food stores. You can use your favourite fruit chutney instead.

fish cutlets with **pesto** butter

80g butter, softened
2 tablespoons basil pesto
1 teaspoon finely grated
   lemon rind
4 x 200g white fish cutlets

preparation and cooking time
20 minutes
serves 4
nutritional count per serving
23.8g total fat (12.8g saturated fat);
1459kJ (349 cal); 0.3g carbohydrate;
33.7g protein; 0.3g fibre

1 Stir butter, pesto and rind in small bowl until well combined.
2 Cook fish in heated oiled large frying pan until cooked through. Remove from pan.
3 Place butter mixture in same pan; stir over low heat until butter melts. Return fish to pan; turn to coat in butter mixture. Serve fish with baby spinach leaves, if desired.

We used blue-eye cutlets, but you can use any white fish cutlets you like.

oven-steamed ocean trout

4 x 200g ocean trout fillets
2 tablespoons lemon juice
1 tablespoon rinsed, drained
  capers, chopped coarsely
2 teaspoons coarsely chopped
  fresh dill

preparation and cooking time
25 minutes
serves 4
nutritional count per serving
7.6g total fat (1.8g saturated fat);
957kJ (229 cal); 0.6g carbohydrate;
38.9g protein; 0.1g fibre

1 Preheat oven to 200°C/180°C fan-forced.
2 Place each fillet on a square of foil large enough to completely enclose fish; top with equal amounts of juice, capers and dill. Gather corners of foil squares together above fish, twist to close securely.
3 Place foil parcels on oven tray; cook about 15 minutes or until fish is cooked as desired.
4 Serve fish parcels with boiled potatoes, if you like.

mussels in thai broth

1kg medium black mussels
¼ cup (75g) red curry paste
400ml can coconut milk
1 cup firmly packed fresh
  coriander leaves

preparation and cooking time
35 minutes
serves 4
nutritional count per serving
27.2g total fat (19g saturated fat);
1325kJ (317 cal); 7.8g carbohydrate;
9.1g protein; 3.9g fibre

1 Scrub mussels; remove beards.
2 Cook curry paste in heated oiled wok, stirring, until fragrant. Add coconut milk and 2½ cups water; bring to the boil. Reduce heat; simmer, covered, 10 minutes or until broth thickens slightly.
3 Add mussels; simmer, covered, about 5 minutes or until mussels open (discard any that do not).
4 Serve bowls of soup sprinkled with coriander.

tip Macadamia nuts are native to Australia but grown and eaten around the globe. They're little perfect spheres of goodness, with a delicate flavour and a crunchy texture containing a high percentage of the "good" monounsaturated fats.

tip Salmon is an important inclusion in your weekly diet because it is low in kilojoules and saturated fat and high in protein. It's also a rich source of omega-3 essential fatty acids plus niacin and vitamin B12. To make your own mayonnaise, see page 156.

fish in macadamia butter

½ cup macadamias
80g butter
⅓ cup finely chopped
    fresh coriander
4 x 200g white fish fillets

preparation and cooking time
15 minutes
serves 4
nutritional count per serving
34.1g total fat (14g saturated fat);
2006kJ (480 cal); 1g carbohydrate;
42.4g protein; 1.2g fibre
We used bream fillets, but you can
use any firm white fish fillets you like.

1 Dry-fry nuts in large frying pan over low heat, shaking pan constantly, until fragrant; remove from heat. When cool enough to handle, chop nuts coarsely.
2 Melt butter in same pan; cook nuts and coriander, stirring, 1 minute. Add fish; cook, turning halfway through cooking time, until cooked through.
3 Drizzle fish with butter. Serve with steamed baby green beans, if desired.

salmon with wasabi mayonnaise

4 x 200g salmon fillets, skin on
½ cup (150g) mayonnaise
2 teaspoons wasabi paste
1 teaspoon finely chopped
    fresh coriander

preparation and cooking time
20 minutes
serves 4
nutritional count per serving
5.6g total fat (9.1g saturated fat);
3553kJ (850 cal); 15.5g carbohydrate;
78.9g protein; 0.8g fibre

1 Cook fish, skin-side down, in heated oiled large frying pan until skin crisps. Turn fish; cook, uncovered, until cooked as desired.
2 Meanwhile, combine mayonnaise, wasabi and coriander in small bowl.
3 Serve fish with wasabi mayonnaise and, if desired, watercress and lime wedges.

almond crumbed fish

¼ cup (20g) finely grated
   parmesan cheese
1 cup (120g) almond meal
2 eggs
4 x 275g white fish fillets

preparation and cooking time
35 minutes
serves 4
nutritional count per serving
26.9g total fat (4.8g saturated fat);
2182kJ (522 cal); 1.4g carbohydrate;
67.3g protein; 2.6g fibre

1 Preheat oven to 240°C/220°C fan-forced.
2 Combine cheese and almond meal in medium shallow bowl; beat eggs in another medium shallow bowl.
3 Coat fish all over in egg, then coat in almond mixture. Place fish, in single layer, on oiled oven tray; spray with cooking-oil spray. Cook fish, uncovered, about 20 minutes or until cooked as desired.

We used snapper fillets, but you can use any firm white fish fillets you like.

fast fish vindaloo

4 x 200g white fish fillets, skin on
1 large brown onion (200g),
   sliced thinly
¼ cup (75g) vindaloo curry paste
2 medium tomatoes (300g),
   chopped coarsely

preparation and cooking time
30 minutes
serves 4
nutritional count per serving
10.4g total fat (2g saturated fat);
1237kJ (296 cal); 5.5g carbohydrate;
43.2g protein; 3.5g fibre

1 Cook fish in heated oiled large frying pan, skin-side down, until browned. Turn; cook other side until browned. Remove from pan.
2 Cook onion in same pan, stirring, until onion softens. Add curry paste; cook, stirring, until fragrant. Add tomato and 1 cup water; bring to the boil. Reduce heat; simmer, uncovered, 5 minutes.
3 Return fish to pan; simmer, uncovered, about 5 minutes or until fish is cooked through. If you like, sprinkle vindaloo with coriander leaves and serve with steamed rice and yogurt.

We used blue-eye fillets, but any firm white fish fillets, such as cod, can be used.

fish with antipasto salad

4 white fish cutlets (800g)
2 x 280g jars antipasto
  vegetables, drained
½ cup fresh flat-leaf
  parsley leaves
1 large red onion (300g),
  sliced thinly

preparation and cooking time
15 minutes
serves 4
nutritional count per serving
5.5g total fat (1.6g saturated fat);
1020kJ (244 cal); 10.2g carbohydrate;
36.3g protein; 3.9g fibre

1 Cook fish in heated oiled large frying pan until browned both sides and cooked through.
2 Meanwhile, combine antipasto vegetables with parsley and onion in medium bowl. Serve fish with antipasto mixture, and lemon wedges, if desired.

Use any firm white fish fillets you like: blue eye, bream, swordfish, cod, halibut, ling or whiting are all good choices.

ginger and kaffir lime fish parcels

4 x 180g white fish fillets
3 green onions, sliced thinly
5cm piece fresh ginger (25g),
  sliced thinly
4 fresh kaffir lime leaves,
  shredded finely

preparation and cooking time
20 minutes
serves 4
nutritional count per serving
4g total fat (1.3g saturated fat);
789kJ (188 cal); 0.6g carbohydrate;
36.9g protein; 0.3g fibre

1 Preheat oven to 180°C/160°C fan-forced.
2 Place fillets on large square of oiled foil or baking paper; top with onion, ginger and lime leaves. Gather corners together; fold to enclose.
3 Place parcels on oven trays; cook about 15 minutes or until fish is cooked through.
4 Remove fish from parcel, discard topping from fish. Serve fish with lime wedges and steamed jasmine rice, if desired.

We used perch fillets, but you can use any firm white fish fillets you like.

spiced fried fish

1½ teaspoons ground cumin
1 teaspoon sweet smoked paprika
¼ teaspoon cayenne pepper
8 white fish fillets (800g)

preparation and cooking time
20 minutes
serves 4
nutritional count per serving
4.4g total fat (1.4g saturated fat);
857kJ (205 cal); 0g carbohydrate;
40.8g protein; 0g fibre
We used bream fillets, but you can
use any firm white fish fillets you like.

1 Combine spices in medium bowl, add fish; rub
spice mixture all over fish.
2 Cook fish in heated oiled large frying pan until
browned and cooked as desired. Serve fish with
lemon wedges, if desired.

ocean trout with anchovy

60g butter
4 drained anchovy fillets,
    chopped finely
2 tablespoons flaked almonds
4 x 200g ocean trout

preparation and cooking time
15 minutes
serves 4
nutritional count per serving
25.7g total fat (10.3g saturated fat);
1680kJ (402 cal); 0.5g carbohydrate;
42g protein; 0.9g fibre

1 Heat butter in large frying pan; add anchovy
and nuts. Cook, stirring, 2 minutes or until nuts
are browned lightly.
2 Add fish; cook, covered, about 5 minutes or
until cooked as desired.
3 Serve fish with lemon wedges and sprinkled
with chopped parsley, if desired.

rigatoni marinara

2 x 425g cans crushed tomatoes
500g marinara mix,
  chopped coarsely
¼ cup coarsely chopped
  fresh flat-leaf parsley
375g rigatoni

preparation and cooking time
20 minutes
serves 4
nutritional count per serving
5.1g total fat (1.2g saturated fat);
2182kJ (522 cal); 71.8g carbohydrate;
43g protein; 5.8g fibre

1 Bring undrained tomatoes to the boil in oiled large frying pan. Reduce heat; simmer, uncovered, about 10 minutes or until tomato thickens slightly.
2 Add marinara mix; cook, stirring occasionally, about 3 minutes or until seafood is cooked through. Stir in parsley.
3 Meanwhile, cook pasta in large saucepan of boiling water, uncovered, until just tender; drain. Toss pasta through hot sauce.

tip Marinara mix is a mixture of uncooked, chopped seafood (most often prawns, salmon, calamari, mussels and flake); it is available from fish markets and some major supermarkets.

steamed salmon with burnt orange sauce

1 large orange (300g)
½ cup (110g) caster sugar
1 tablespoon rice wine vinegar
4 x 200g salmon fillets

preparation and cooking time
35 minutes
serves 4
nutritional count per serving
14.2g total fat (3.2g saturated fat); 1735kJ (415 cal); 31.3g carbohydrate; 39.5g protein; 1g fibre

1 Grate rind from orange (you need 1 teaspoon). Juice orange (you need ¼ cup).
2 Combine sugar and ⅓ cup water in heated small saucepan; stir, without boiling, until sugar dissolves. Bring to the boil; reduce heat. Simmer, uncovered, without stirring, until mixture is a light caramel colour.
3 Remove pan from heat; allow bubbles to subside. Carefully stir in rind and juice; return pan to low heat. Stir until any pieces of caramel melt. Remove pan from heat; stir in vinegar.
4 Meanwhile, place fish in large bamboo steamer set over large saucepan of simmering water; steam, covered, 15 minutes. Drizzle fish with sauce; serve with watercress, if desired.

tar-crumbed lamb backstrap

2 tablespoons za'atar
⅓ cup coarsely chopped
  roasted unsalted cashews
800g lamb backstraps
2 tablespoons olive oil

preparation and cooking time
15 minutes
serves 4
nutritional count per serving
24.7g total fat (5.7g saturated fat);
1701kJ (407 cal); 2.2g carbohydrate;
44g protein; 1.2g fibre

1 Blend or process za'atar and nuts until mixture resembles coarse breadcrumbs.
2 Combine lamb with oil in large bowl; add za'atar mixture, turn lamb to coat all over.
3 Cook lamb, in batches, in heated oiled large frying pan, until cooked as desired. Cover; stand 5 minutes then slice thickly. Serve with lemon wedges and spinach couscous, if you like.

moroccan lamb cutlets

12 lamb cutlets (900g), trimmed
2 tablespoons moroccan seasoning
2 tablespoons coarsely chopped
  fresh coriander
2 tablespoons olive oil

preparation and cooking time
15 minutes
serves 4
nutritional count per serving
28.4g total fat (10.1g saturated fat);
1463kJ (350 cal); 1.2g carbohydrate;
22.9g protein; 0.3g fibre

1 Combine ingredients in large bowl. Toss lamb to coat in mixture.
2 Cook lamb in heated oiled large frying pan until browned both sides and cooked as desired.

slow-roasted mushrooms

We used oyster, shiitake, swiss brown and flat mushrooms for this recipe.

800g mixed mushrooms,
   chopped coarsely
300g vine-ripened tomatoes,
   chopped coarsely
1 small red onion (100g),
   sliced thinly
1 tablespoon olive oil

1 Preheat oven to 160°C/140°C fan-forced.
2 Combine ingredients in large baking dish; roast, uncovered, about 40 minutes or until mushrooms are tender.
3 If you like, serve the mushrooms with soft polenta and sprinkle with chopped chives.

preparation and cooking time
50 minutes
serves 4
nutritional count per serving
5.2g total fat (0.6g saturated fat);
443kJ (106 cal); 3.4g carbohydrate;
8.3g protein; 62g fibre

cauliflower and pumpkin curry

2 tablespoons yellow curry paste
500g pumpkin, chopped coarsely
½ small cauliflower (500g),
   cut into florets
200g natural yogurt

1 Cook curry paste in heated oiled large saucepan until fragrant. Add pumpkin; cook, stirring, 2 minutes. Add 1½ cups water; bring to the boil. Reduce heat; simmer, uncovered, 5 minutes.
2 Add cauliflower; simmer, uncovered, 10 minutes or until vegetables are just tender. Add yogurt; stir over low heat until hot. Serve with steamed rice and lemon wedges, if desired.

preparation and cooking time
35 minutes
serves 4
nutritional count per serving
5.9g total fat (1.8g saturated fat);
602kJ (144 cal); 12.4g carbohydrate;
7.9g protein; 4.7g fibre

lamb cutlets with sweet citrus sauce

8 lamb cutlets (600g)
1 large orange (300g)
½ cup (160g) redcurrant jelly
1 tablespoon red wine vinegar

preparation and cooking time
25 minutes
serves 4
nutritional count per serving
13.8g total fat (6.3g saturated fat);
1296kJ (310 cal); 28.9g carbohydrate;
16.7g protein; 1.2g fibre

1 Cook lamb in heated oiled large frying pan until cooked as desired.
2 Meanwhile, grate rind from orange (you need 1 teaspoon). Juice orange (you need ⅓ cup).
3 Combine rind, juice, jelly and vinegar in medium saucepan; stir over heat until jelly melts. Bring to the boil; reduce heat. Simmer, uncovered, until sauce thickens slightly.
4 Serve lamb with citrus sauce; accompany with mashed potatoes and rocket, if desired.

hoisin sweet chilli lamb and vegetable stir-fry

750g lamb strips
400g packaged fresh stir-fry
  vegetables
⅓ cup (80ml) hoisin sauce
2 tablespoons sweet chilli sauce

preparation and cooking time
15 minutes
serves 4
nutritional count per serving
18.2g total fat (7.7g saturated fat);
1689kJ (404 cal); 14.6g carbohydrate;
41.8g protein; 7.5g fibre

1 Stir-fry lamb, in batches, in heated oiled wok until cooked through.
2 Stir-fry vegetables in wok until almost tender. Return lamb to wok with sauces and 2 tablespoons water; stir-fry until hot.

tip Lamb cutlets are a great source of protein and the combination here of the meat with the delicately tangy flavour of the citrus sauce is a treat for your taste buds.

tip Make sure the wok is very hot and continue to stir continuously while cooking. Don't overcook the vegetables – they should remain slightly crunchy, not soft.

34

Weekend Barbecues

Everyone's relaxed and the drifting aromas from the barbecue hotplate are heavenly. Gather your friends and family, because here are some ideas to make your next barbecue sizzle.

salt and pepper paprika prawns

24 uncooked medium
  king prawns (1kg)
2 teaspoons sweet paprika
2 teaspoons sea salt
1 teaspoon cracked black pepper

preparation and cooking time
25 minutes
makes 24
nutritional count per prawn
0.1g total fat (0g saturated fat);
79kJ (19 cal); 0g carbohydrate;
4.3g protein; 0g fibre

1 Shell and devein prawns, leaving tails intact. Combine paprika, salt and pepper in medium bowl; add prawns, toss to coat in mixture.
2 Cook prawns, in batches, on heated oiled grill plate (or grill or barbecue) until changed in colour.
3 Serve prawns with your favourite dipping sauce, if you like.

mini scallop and lime kebabs

24 scallops (600g), roe removed
3 cloves garlic, crushed
3 limes
12 fresh kaffir lime leaves,
  halved lengthways

preparation and cooking time
20 minutes (plus refrigeration time)
makes 24
nutritional count per scallop
0.2g total fat (0.1g saturated fat);
63kJ (15 cal); 0.3g carbohydrate;
3g protein; 0.2g fibre
You need 24 strong toothpicks.

1 Combine scallops and garlic in medium bowl, cover; refrigerate 30 minutes.
2 Meanwhile, cut each lime into eight wedges. Skewer one piece of lime leaf and one lime wedge onto each toothpick.
3 Cook scallops on oiled grill plate (or grill or barbecue) about 5 minutes or until cooked as desired. Stand 5 minutes then skewer one scallop onto each toothpick.

tip Paprika is made from ground dried sweet red and green capsicums and comes in a range of colours and strengths. Paradoxically, the reddest paprika is the mildest, while light brown paprika is the hottest. Sweet paprika is mid-way along the spectrum.

tip Scallops can be bought fresh or frozen and their soft, fleshy texture makes them perfect for kebabs. They're not only irresistibly sweet; they are also a very good source of vitamin B12 and omega-3 fatty acids. Be careful not to overcook them as they can toughen.

prawn and chorizo skewers

24 uncooked medium
  king prawns (1kg)
8 x 20cm stalks fresh rosemary
4 cloves garlic, sliced thinly
2 chorizo sausages (340g),
  sliced thickly

preparation and cooking time
25 minutes
serves 4
nutritional count per serving
26.3g total fat (9.4g saturated fat);
1739kJ (416 cal); 2.5g carbohydrate;
42.3g protein; 0.8g fibre

1 Shell and devein prawns, leaving tails intact.
2 Remove leaves from bottom two-thirds of each rosemary stalk; thread prawns, garlic and chorizo, alternately, onto rosemary skewers.
3 Cook skewers in heated oiled grill pan (or grill or barbecue) until prawns are just changed in colour and chorizo is browned.

tandoori lamb cutlets

¼ cup (75g) tandoori paste
¼ cup (70g) yogurt
1 tablespoon lemon juice
12 french-trimmed lamb cutlets
  (600g)

preparation and cooking time
20 minutes
serves 4
nutritional count per serving
20.2g total fat (7.3g saturated fat);
1112kJ (266 cal); 2.4g carbohydrate;
18.1g protein; 1.9g fibre

1 Combine ingredients in large bowl; turn to coat lamb in tandoori mixture.
2 Cook lamb on heated oiled grill plate (or grill or barbecue) until browned both sides and cooked as desired.

teriyaki lamb skewers

2 tablespoons japanese soy sauce
2 tablespoons mirin
600g diced lamb
9 green onions

preparation and cooking time
35 minutes
serves 4
nutritional count per serving
13.3g total fat (6g saturated fat);
1083kJ (259 cal); 1.2g carbohydrate;
32.2g protein; 0.3g fibre

1 Combine sauce, mirin and lamb in medium bowl.
2 Cut four 3cm-long pieces from trimmed root end of each onion.
3 Thread lamb and onion pieces, alternately, onto skewers; cook on heated oiled grill plate (or grill or barbecue), brushing with soy mixture occasionally, until lamb is cooked as desired.

sesame and chilli lamb

½ cup toasted sesame seeds
½ teaspoon dried chilli flakes
800g lamb backstraps
2 tablespoons olive oil

preparation and cooking time
35 minutes
serves 4
nutritional count per serving
26g total fat (5.7g saturated fat);
1739kJ (416 cal); 0.2g carbohydrate;
44.9g protein; 1.8g fibre

1 Combine ingredients in large bowl; turn lamb to coat in mixture.
2 Cook lamb on heated oiled grill plate (or grill or barbecue) until browned and cooked as desired. Cover; stand 5 minutes then slice thickly.

tip Fennel is popular in French, Italian and Greek cooking and has a sweet licorice flavour. The entire fennel plant (bulb, stalks and leaves) is edible. The stalks can be used in soups and stews and the leaves (also known as fronds) can be used as a herb, providing great flavour to baked fish and poultry.

tip Mirin is a sweet rice wine used in Japanese cooking. There are two types of Mirin – Hon Mirin with an alcohol level of 14% and Shin Mirin containing less than 1% alcohol – and they are widely available in supermarkets and Asian grocery stores. We use Shin Mirin in our recipes, unless otherwise stated.

veal chops with grilled fennel and mandarin

4 x 200g veal chops
2 baby fennel bulbs (260g),
   trimmed, halved lengthways
4 small mandarins (400g), peeled,
   halved horizontally
2 tablespoons prepared basil pesto

preparation and cooking time
25 minutes
cooking time 20 minutes
serves 4
nutritional count per serving
7.8g total fat (2g saturated fat);
1070kJ (256 cal); 7g carbohydrate;
37.9g protein; 2.7g fibre

1 Cook veal on heated oiled grill plate (or grill or barbecue) until cooked.
2 Cook fennel and mandarin on grill plate until just browned.
3 Top veal with pesto; serve with fennel and mandarin.

chicken yakitori

500g chicken breast fillets
½ cup (125ml) mirin
¼ cup (60ml) kecap manis
1 teaspoon toasted sesame seeds

preparation and cooking time
30 minutes (plus refrigeration time)
makes 24
nutritional count per skewer
1.2g total fat (0.4g saturated fat);
128kJ (33 cal); 0.2g carbohydrate;
4.6g protein; 0g fibre
You need 24 bamboo skewers for this recipe. Soak in water for at least an hour before using to avoid scorching and splintering during cooking.

1 Slice chicken into thin diagonal strips; thread strips loosely onto skewers. Place skewers, in single layer, in large shallow dish.
2 Combine mirin and kecap manis in small jug. Pour half the marinade over skewers; reserve remaining marinade. Cover; refrigerate 3 hours or overnight.
3 Simmer reserved marinade in small saucepan over low heat until reduced by half.
4 Meanwhile, cook drained skewers on heated oiled grill plate (or grill or barbecue) until chicken is cooked through.
5 Serve skewers drizzled with hot marinade and sprinkled with sesame seeds.

spanish-style barbecued leg of lamb

2.5kg leg of lamb
2 chorizo sausages (340g),
  chopped coarsely
10 cloves garlic, halved
1 tablespoon sweet paprika

preparation and cooking time
1 hour 50 minutes
(plus standing time)
serves 10
nutritional count per serving
20.2g total fat (8.2g saturated fat);
1572kJ (376 cal); 1g carbohydrate;
47.5g protein; 0.3g fibre

1 Place lamb in large baking dish, make deep slits all over with sharp knife; push sausage and garlic into slits. Sprinkle with paprika.
2 Cook lamb in covered barbecue, following manufacturer's instructions, using indirect heat, about 1 hour 40 minutes or until cooked as desired. Cover lamb; stand 20 minutes before serving.

barbecued scotch fillet

¼ cup (60ml) barbecue sauce
2 tablespoons american mustard
½ cup (125ml) beer
1.4kg piece beef scotch fillet

preparation and cooking time
1 hour 40 minutes
(plus refrigeration and standing time)
serves 6
nutritional count per serving
14.2g total fat (5.8g saturated fat);
1484kJ (355 cal); 5.6g carbohydrate;
49.6g protein; 0.3g fibre

1 Combine sauce, mustard and beer in large bowl; add beef, turn to coat in mixture. Cover; refrigerate 3 hours or overnight.
2 Place beef and marinade in oiled disposable aluminium baking dish. Cook beef in covered barbecue, following manufacturer's instructions, using indirect heat, about 1½ hours or until cooked as desired. Cover; stand 15 minutes then slice thinly.

sumac lamb loin chops

1 clove garlic, crushed
1 tablespoon sumac
2 teaspoons ground coriander
8 lamb loin chops (800g)

1 Combine garlic, spices and 2 tablespoons water in medium bowl, add lamb; toss lamb to coat in mixture.
2 Cook lamb on heated oiled grill plate (or grill or barbecue) until cooked as desired.

preparation and cooking time
45 minutes
serves 4
nutritional count per serving
20.3g total fat (9.2g saturated fat); 1275kJ (305 cal); 0.1g carbohydrate; 30.8g protein; 0.1g fibre

lamb chops with capsicum mayonnaise

100g roasted capsicum
½ cup (150g) mayonnaise
8 lamb mid-loin chops (800g)

1 Blend or process capsicum and mayonnaise until smooth.
2 Cook lamb, in batches, on heated oiled grill plate (or grill or barbecue) until browned all over and cooked as desired.
3 Top lamb with capsicum mayonnaise; serve with mashed potato, if desired.

preparation and cooking time
25 minutes
serves 4
nutritional count per serving
34.1g total fat (10.7g saturated fat); 1927kJ (461 cal); 7.8g carbohydrate; 31.4g protein; 0.2g fibre

chilli-rubbed hickory-smoked rib-eye steaks

You need 100g hickory smoking chips and a smoke box, available at most barbecue supply stores.

1 tablespoon finely grated
  lemon rind
2 teaspoons chilli powder
2 tablespoons olive oil
4 x 200g beef rib-eye steaks

preparation and cooking time
20 minutes
(plus refrigeration and standing time)
serves 4
nutritional count per serving
22.1g total fat (6.9g saturated fat);
1589kJ (380 cal); 0.1g carbohydrate;
45.2g protein; 0.1g fibre

1 Combine rind, chilli and oil in large bowl with steaks. Cover; refrigerate 3 hours or overnight.
2 Cover smoking chips with 2 cups water in medium bowl; stand 3 hours or overnight.
3 Place drained smoking chips in smoke box alongside steaks on grill plate. Cook steaks in covered barbecue, following manufacturer's instructions, using indirect heat, about 10 minutes or until cooked.

barbecue and honey steak

2 tablespoons barbecue sauce
1 tablespoon worcestershire sauce
1 tablespoon honey
4 x 200g new-york cut
  beef steaks

preparation and cooking time
25 minutes
serves 4
nutritional count per serving
12g total fat (5g saturated fat);
1363kJ (326 cal); 11.8g carbohydrate;
42.4g protein; 0.2g fibre

1 Combine sauces and honey in large bowl, add beef; turn to coat in mixture.
2 Cook beef on heated oiled grill plate (or grill or barbecue) until browned both sides and cooked as desired.

barbecued pork spareribs with plum and star anise

1 cup (250ml) plum sauce
⅓ cup (80ml) oyster sauce
3 star anise
2kg slabs american-style
   pork spareribs

preparation and cooking time
45 minutes (plus refrigeration time)
serves 4
nutritional count per serving
18.9g total fat (6.1g saturated fat);
2387kJ (571 cal); 50.7g carbohydrate;
48.5g protein; 0.5g fibre

1 Combine sauces and star anise in medium saucepan; bring to the boil. Remove from heat; cool 10 minutes.
2 Place pork in large shallow baking dish; brush marinade all over pork. Pour remaining marinade over pork, cover; refrigerate 3 hours or overnight, turning pork occasionally.
3 Drain pork; reserve marinade. Cook pork on heated oiled grill plate (or grill or barbecue) about 30 minutes or until cooked through, turning and brushing frequently with some of the reserved marinade.
4 Boil remaining marinade in small saucepan about 5 minutes or until thickened slightly.
5 Slice spareribs into portions; serve with hot marinade.

veal cutlets with onion marmalade

2 large red onions (600g),
   sliced thinly
⅓ cup (75g) firmly packed
   brown sugar
¼ cup (60ml) cider vinegar
4 veal cutlets (680g)

preparation and cooking time
35 minutes
serves 4
nutritional count per serving
3.5g total fat (1g saturated fat);
1137kJ (272 cal); 26.2g carbohydrate;
32.7g protein; 2g fibre

1 Cook onion in heated oiled medium saucepan, stirring, until soft and browned lightly. Add sugar and vinegar; cook, stirring, about 15 minutes or until onion caramelises.
2 Cook veal on heated oiled grill plate (or grill or barbecue) until cooked as desired. Serve veal topped with onion marmalade.

char-grilled steak with baba ghanoush

4 x 150g beef eye-fillet steaks
2 medium red capsicums (400g),
  sliced thickly
2 large zucchini (300g), sliced
  thinly lengthways
½ cup (120g) baba ghanoush

preparation and cooking time
35 minutes
serves 4
nutritional count per serving
10.6g total fat (3.9g saturated fat);
1091kJ (261 cal); 5.3g carbohydrate;
34.6g protein; 3.1g fibre

1 Spray steaks and vegetables with cooking-oil spray. Cook steaks and vegetables on heated grill plate (or grill or barbecue), in batches, until steaks are cooked as desired and vegetables are tender.
2 Divide vegetables among serving plates, top with steaks. Serve with baba ghanoush, and fresh mint leaves, if desired.

scotch fillet in barbecue sauce

2 tablespoons brown sugar
2 tablespoons barbecue sauce
2 tablespoons tomato sauce
4 x 200g beef scotch fillet steaks

preparation and cooking time
35 minutes
serves 4
nutritional count per serving
12g total fat (5g saturated fat);
1400kJ (335 cal); 13.8g carbohydrate;
42.4g protein; 0.3g fibre

1 Combine sugar and sauces in large bowl. Add steaks; turn to coat mixture.
2 Cook steaks on heated oiled grill plate (or grill or barbecue) until cooked as desired. Cover; stand 5 minutes before serving. Serve with grilled corn cobs, if desired.

tip Considered a cut above the rest, eye fillet (or tenderloin) steaks are the most tender cut of beef. They are best cooked hot and fast.

tip Also known as the rib eye, the scotch fillet is a cut of steak from the beef rib where the meat is tender and fattier (marbled). This natural marbling makes it very juicy, flavoursome and easy to cook.

harissa and lime-rubbed pork

1 lime
½ cup (120g) harissa paste
1 clove garlic, crushed
600g pork fillets

preparation and cooking time
30 minutes
serves 4
nutritional count per serving
12.9g total fat (2.2g saturated fat);
1133kJ (271 cal); 2.5g carbohydrate;
34.6g protein; 3.4g fibre

1 Grate rind from lime (you need 2 teaspoons). Juice lime (you need 1 tablespoon).
2 Combine harissa, rind, juice, garlic and pork in large bowl.
3 Cook pork, uncovered, on heated oiled grill plate (or grill or barbecue) until browned all over. Cover pork; cook about 10 minutes or until cooked as desired. Cover pork, stand 5 minutes then slice thickly.

roast peppered pork

1 tablespoon coarse cooking salt
1 tablespoon drained
   canned green peppercorns
   in brine, crushed
2 tablespoons mixed dried
   peppercorns, crushed
1kg piece pork shoulder

preparation and cooking time
1 hour 40 minutes
serves 6
nutritional count per serving
13.4g total fat (4.5g saturated fat);
1120kJ (268 cal); 10g carbohydrate;
35.6g protein; 0.6g fibre

1 Combine salt and peppercorns in small bowl.
2 Score pork rind; spray pork with cooking-oil spray. Rub pepper mixture over pork.
3 Cook pork in disposable aluminium baking dish, in covered barbecue, following manufacturer's instructions, using indirect heat, about 1½ hours or until cooked through.
4 Cover pork; stand 10 minutes then slice thickly.

piri-piri chicken thigh fillets

¼ cup (60ml) bottled piri-piri sauce
2 tablespoons olive oil
2 teaspoons brown sugar
8 x 125g chicken thigh fillets

1 Combine ingredients in medium bowl.
2 Cook chicken on heated oiled grill plate (or grill or barbecue) until cooked through. Serve with lime wedges, if desired.

preparation and cooking time
20 minutes
serves 4
nutritional count per serving
27.5g total fat (6.9g saturated fat);
1885kJ (451 cal); 4.5g carbohydrate;
46.6g protein; 0.7g fibre

sesame wasabi chicken

1 tablespoon japanese soy sauce
1 tablespoon sesame oil
2 tablespoons wasabi paste
8 chicken drumsticks (1.2kg)

1 Combine sauce, oil and wasabi in large bowl, add chicken; turn to coat in mixture.
2 Cook chicken on heated oiled flat plate (or grill or barbecue), turning and brushing occasionally with marinade, about 40 minutes or until cooked through.

preparation and cooking time
50 minutes
serves 4
nutritional count per serving
25.6g total fat (7g saturated fat);
1551kJ (371 cal); 1.2g carbohydrate;
34.1g protein; 0.8g fibre

thai red curry chicken

2 tablespoons red curry paste
⅓ cup loosely packed fresh
   coriander leaves
½ cup (125ml) coconut milk
4 x 200g chicken breast fillets

preparation and cooking time
20 minutes
serves 4
nutritional count per serving
12.8g total fat (6.9g saturated fat);
727kJ (174 cal); 2.2g carbohydrate;
12g protein; 1.8g fibre

1 Blend or process curry paste, coriander and coconut milk until smooth. Combine curry mixture and chicken in medium bowl; toss to coat chicken in mixture.
2 Cook chicken on heated oiled flat plate until browned both sides. Cover; cook 10 minutes or until cooked through.
3 If you like, sprinkle the chicken with coriander and serve with steamed jasmine rice.

fontina, pancetta and sage chicken

1 bunch fresh sage
4 x 200g chicken breast fillets
4 thin slices fontina cheese (100g)
4 slices pancetta (60g)

preparation and cooking time
35 minutes
serves 4
nutritional count per serving
20.6g total fat (8.9g saturated fat);
1655kJ (396 cal); 0.1g carbohydrate;
52.8g protein; 0g fibre
Instead of fontina, try gruyere, edam, emmental or gouda cheese.

1 Reserve 16 sage leaves. Chop remaining sage coarsely (you need 1 tablespoon). Make a pocket in one side of each fillet but do not cut all the way through. Divide cheese, pancetta and chopped sage among pockets; secure with toothpicks.
2 Cook chicken on heated oiled grill plate (or grill or barbecue), about 20 minutes or until cooked through. Remove toothpicks before serving.
3 Cook whole sage leaves on oiled grill plate until browned lightly. Serve chicken topped with sage leaves.

salmon with pistachio mayonnaise

4 x 200g salmon fillets, skin on
⅓ cup (80g) mayonnaise
2 tablespoons lemon juice
⅓ cup (45g) roasted pistachios,
  chopped coarsely

1 Cook salmon on heated oiled grill plate (or grill or barbecue), skin-side down, until skin is crisp; turn, cook until cooked as desired.
2 Meanwhile, combine mayonnaise, juice and nuts in medium bowl.
3 Serve salmon topped with pistachio mayonnaise.

preparation and cooking time
20 minutes
serves 4
nutritional count per serving
26.4g total fat (4.6g saturated fat);
1789kJ (428 cal); 6g carbohydrate;
41.5g protein; 1.1g fibre

grilled spiced haloumi

1 tablespoon olive oil
1 tablespoon moroccan seasoning
1 teaspoon grated lemon rind
250g haloumi cheese

1 Combine oil, seasoning and rind in medium bowl, add haloumi; toss to coat in mixture.
2 Cook haloumi on heated oiled grill plate (or grill or barbecue) until browned both sides. Serve with lemon wedges, if you like.

preparation and cooking time
20 minutes
serves 4
nutritional count per serving
15.3g total fat (7.5g saturated fat);
823kJ (197 cal); 1.7g carbohydrate;
13.4g protein; 0.2g fibre
Haloumi should be eaten while still warm as it becomes tough and rubbery on cooling.

tip There are a number of fish that qualify as "white fish" including cod, whiting, haddock, hake, bass (silver bass, sea bass and striped bass) and several fish that come under the banner of "bream". White fish don't have the omega-3 content of oily fish, but they have lower levels of contaminants like mercury.

tip We made a very simple warm bean salad to go with this recipe. Cook 1 thinly sliced small red onion and 1 coarsely chopped large tomato in a heated medium saucepan until soft. Add a 420g can of rinsed, drained kidney beans and stir until mixture is heated through.

fish with ginger & orange

2 tablespoons orange marmalade
1 tablespoon kecap manis
3cm piece fresh ginger (15g),
    grated
4 x 200g white fish fillets

preparation and cooking time
30 minutes
serves 4
nutritional count per serving
4.4g total fat (1.4g saturated fat);
978kJ (234 cal); 6.9g carbohydrate;
41.1g protein; 0.2g fibre

1 Combine marmalade, kecap manis and ginger in small bowl.
2 Cook fish on heated oiled flat plate until browned both sides. Pour marmalade mixture over fish; cook, spooning sauce over fish, until fish is cooked as desired.
3 If you like, serve fish with fresh lime slices and fresh rice noodles stir-fried with grated zucchini and cabbage.

We used blue-eye fillets in this recipe, but you can use any firm white fish fillets you like.

cajun-style fish

2 tablespoons cajun seasoning
2 teaspoons grated lemon rind
1 tablespoon vegetable oil
4 x 200g white fish fillets

preparation and cooking time
20 minutes
serves 4
nutritional count per serving
9.1g total fat (2g saturated fat);
1058kJ (253 cal); 1.2g carbohydrate;
41g protein; 0.4g fibre

1 Combine seasoning, rind and oil in small bowl. Rub mixture over fish.
2 Cook fish on heated oiled grill plate (or grill or barbecue) until just cooked through. Serve fish with coleslaw or salad, if you like.

We used kingfish fillets in this recipe, but you can use any firm white fish fillets you like.

34

Sunday Night

You want the weekend to keep going. It's Sunday night and you don't want to think about work. You want easy, comforting, delicious food that is as relaxed as you are.

cream of kumara soup

2 medium kumara (800g),
chopped coarsely
1 medium brown onion (150g),
chopped coarsely
2 cups (500ml) vegetable stock
½ cup (125ml) cream

preparation and cooking time
30 minutes (plus cooling time)
serves 6
nutritional count per serving
9.5g total fat (6.1g saturated fat);
748kJ (179 cal); 18.5g carbohydrate;
3.8g protein; 2.4g fibre

1 Cook kumara and onion in heated oiled large saucepan, stirring, 10 minutes. Add stock and 2 cups water; bring to the boil. Reduce heat; simmer, covered, about 15 minutes or until kumara is soft. Cool 15 minutes.
2 Blend or process soup, in batches, until smooth. Return soup to same cleaned pan; stir over medium heat until hot.
3 Drizzle soup with cream; serve with rosemary sourdough (see recipe, below), if you like – it goes really well with this soup.

rosemary sourdough

1 loaf sourdough bread (675g)
2 tablespoons olive oil
2 teaspoons finely chopped
fresh rosemary

preparation and cooking time
20 minutes
serves 6
nutritional count per serving
9g total fat (1.3g saturated fat);
1392kJ (333 cal); 50.3g carbohydrate;
9.7g protein; 5.2g fibre

1 Preheat oven to 180°C/160°C fan-forced.
2 Cut bread into 3cm slices. Combine oil and rosemary in large bowl; add bread, turn to coat in mixture.
3 Place bread on oven tray; toast bread, both sides, about 15 minutes.

right: rosemary sourdough; cream of kumara soup

bubble and squeak

450g potatoes, chopped coarsely
250g cabbage, chopped coarsely
4 rindless bacon rashers (260g),
   chopped coarsely
1 medium brown onion (150g),
   chopped coarsely

preparation and cooking time
40 minutes
serves 4
nutritional count per serving
9.5g total fat (3.4g saturated fat);
957kJ (229 cal); 16.5g carbohydrate;
17.3g protein; 4.3g fibre

1 Boil, steam or microwave potato and cabbage, separately, until just tender; drain. Mash potato in medium bowl until smooth.
2 Meanwhile, cook bacon in heated oiled large frying pan, stirring, until crisp; drain on absorbent paper.
3 Cook onion in same pan, stirring, until softened. Add potato, cabbage and bacon; stir to combine. Flatten mixture to form large cake-shape; cook, uncovered, until bottom of cake is just browned. Carefully invert onto plate, then slide back into frying pan; cook, uncovered, until browned on other side.

chinese chicken and corn soup

2 green chillies, thinly sliced
2 x 505g cans chicken and sweet
   corn soup
3 cups (480g) coarsely chopped
   barbecued chicken
1 egg white

preparation and cooking time
30 minutes
serves 4
nutritional count per serving
9g total fat (2.2g saturated fat);
995kJ (238 cal); 8.1g carbohydrate;
29.8g protein; 2.5g fibre

1 Cook chillies in heated oiled large saucepan about 2 minutes. Add soup, chicken and 2½ cups water; bring to the boil. Reduce heat; simmer.
2 Beat egg white in small jug with 1 tablespoon cold water then slowly pour into soup, stirring constantly. Serve soup sprinkled with sliced green onion, if desired.

cream of spinach soup

3 medium potatoes (600g), chopped coarsely
3 cups (750ml) chicken stock
250g trimmed spinach, chopped coarsely
3/4 cup (180ml) cream

preparation and cooking time
45 minutes (plus cooling time)
serves 6
nutritional count per serving
13.7g total fat (8.8g saturated fat);
832kJ (199 cal); 13.1g carbohydrate;
5g protein; 2.5g fibre

1 Combine potato, stock and 1 litre water in large saucepan; bring to the boil. Reduce heat; simmer, covered, about 15 minutes or until potato is tender. Stir in spinach; cool 15 minutes.
2 Blend or process soup, in batches, until smooth. Return soup to same cleaned pan, add cream; stir over medium heat until hot.
3 Serve bowls of soup with small toasts topped with fetta and finely grated lemon rind, if desired.

thai chicken, pumpkin and coconut soup

1/4 cup (75g) red curry paste
2 x 420g cans cream of pumpkin soup
31/4 cups (760ml) light coconut milk
3 cups (480g) coarsely chopped barbecued chicken

preparation and cooking time
30 minutes
serves 4
nutritional count per serving
38.3g total fat (23.8g saturated fat);
2420kJ (579 cal); 20.9g carbohydrate;
35.7g protein; 4.4g fibre

1 Stir paste in heated large saucepan until fragrant. Add soup, coconut milk and 1½ cups water to the pan; bring to the boil.
2 Stir in the chicken; reduce heat. Simmer until soup is heated through. Serve soup topped with thinly sliced green onion, if desired.

italian tomato and bean soup

420g can condensed tomato soup
85g coarsely chopped roasted
  red capsicum
425g can white beans, rinsed,
  drained
1/3 cup (80ml) cream

1 Blend or process soup, capsicum and 1¾ cups water until smooth.
2 Combine soup mixture in large saucepan with beans; bring to the boil. Reduce heat; simmer, uncovered, about 5 minutes. Stir in cream.
3 Serve bowls of soup sprinkled with fresh baby basil leaves, if desired.

preparation and cooking time
30 minutes
serves 4
nutritional count per serving
9.4g total fat (6g saturated fat);
681kJ (163 cal); 14.5g carbohydrate;
3.5g protein; 3.7g fibre

spaghetti with pesto

375g spaghetti
¼ cup (60g) bottled basil pesto
2 tablespoons lemon juice
¼ cup (35g) coarsely grated
  parmesan cheese

1 Cook pasta in large saucepan of boiling water until tender; drain.
2 Return pasta to pan; add pesto, juice and cheese. Toss to combine.

preparation and cooking time
35 minutes
serves 4
nutritional count per serving
9.9g total fat (3.3g saturated fat);
1747kJ (418 cal); 64.4g carbohydrate;
15.3g protein; 3.4g fibre

pasta alfredo

375g fettuccine
80g butter
300ml cream
½ cup (40g) finely grated
  parmesan cheese

preparation and cooking time
20 minutes

serves 4

nutritional count per serving
53.4g total fat (34.5g saturated fat);
3825kJ (914 cal); 87.5g carbohydrate;
19.4g protein; 4.1g fibre

1 Cook pasta in large saucepan of boiling water until tender; drain.

2 Melt butter in medium frying pan, add cream; bring to the boil. Reduce heat; simmer, uncovered, about 5 minutes or until sauce reduces by half.

3 Add cheese; stir over low heat about 2 minutes or until cheese melts. Remove from heat; add pasta. Toss to coat pasta in sauce.

pasta with pizzaiola sauce

2 x 425g cans crushed tomatoes
2 cloves garlic, crushed
2 tablespoons finely chopped
  fresh oregano
375g spaghetti

preparation and cooking time
45 minutes

serves 4

nutritional count per serving
1.5g total fat (0.2g saturated fat);
1509kJ (361 cal); 70.7g carbohydrate;
12.3g protein; 5.9g fibre

1 Bring undrained tomatoes and garlic to the boil in heated oiled large frying pan. Reduce heat; simmer, uncovered, about 25 minutes or until liquid is reduced by half. Stir in oregano.

2 Meanwhile, cook pasta in large saucepan of boiling water until tender; drain. Remove from heat. Add pasta to sauce; toss pasta to coat in sauce.

tip King Edward potatoes are commonly available. Look for their cream/pale pink skin and creamy-coloured flesh. They have a floury texture and they are excellent for baking, roasting and mashing.

tip This is a great little meal combining all the four food groups in one stomach-satisfying package. You can use refrigerated smoked salmon or canned smoked salmon fillets, located with the tinned fish in the supermarket.

potato and bacon soup

6 rindless bacon rashers (390g),
    chopped coarsely
1kg potatoes, chopped coarsely
1 cup (250ml) chicken stock
1¼ cups (300g) sour cream

preparation and cooking time
15 minutes
serves 6
nutritional count per serving
29.5g total fat (16.6g saturated fat);
1768kJ (423 cal); 20.6g carbohydrate;
18.5g protein; 2.3g fibre

1 Cook bacon, stirring, in heated oiled large
saucepan until bacon is crisp.
2 Add potato, stock and 2 cups water; bring
to the boil. Reduce heat; simmer, covered, until
potato is just tender. Add sour cream; stir until
heated through (do not boil). Remove from heat;
stir in some finely chopped parsley, if you like.

We used King Edward potatoes, but any good
all-purpose potato will be fine.

baked potatoes with salmon and peas

4 large potatoes (1.2kg), unpeeled
½ cup (60g) frozen peas
½ cup (120g) sour cream
100g smoked salmon,
    chopped coarsely

preparation and cooking time
1 hour 20 minutes
serves 4
nutritional count per serving
3.6g total fat (2.2g saturated fat);
405kJ (97 cal); 11.1g carbohydrate;
3.9g protein; 1.9g fibre

1 Preheat oven to 180°C/160°C fan-forced.
2 Pierce potato skins with fork; wrap each
potato in foil, place on oven tray. Bake about
1 hour or until tender.
3 Meanwhile, boil, steam or microwave peas
until tender; drain.
4 Remove potatoes from oven; fold back foil to
reveal tops of potatoes. Increase temperature to
240°C/220°C fan-forced.
5 Cut 1cm from top of each potato; discard.
Carefully scoop out flesh from potatoes, leaving
skins intact. Combine potato flesh with sour
cream in medium bowl; mash potato mixture
until almost smooth. Stir in peas and salmon.
6 Divide potato mixture among potato shells.
Bake about 10 minutes or until browned lightly.

tuna and chilli pasta

375g angel hair pasta
425g can tuna in oil
1 teaspoon dried chilli flakes
400g can chopped tomatoes

preparation and cooking time
25 minutes
serves 4
nutritional count per serving
13g total fat (2.1g saturated fat);
2203kJ (527 cal); 67g carbohydrate;
32.3g protein; 4.3g fibre

1 Cook pasta in large saucepan of boiling water until tender; drain, reserving ¼ cup cooking liquid. Rinse pasta under cold water, drain.
2 Meanwhile, drain tuna, reserving 2 tablespoons of the oil. Heat oil in medium frying pan, add chilli; cook, stirring, 1 minute.
3 Add undrained tomatoes, tuna and reserved cooking liquid to pan; simmer until liquid has reduced slightly. Combine pasta and sauce in large bowl. Serve sprinkled with basil, if desired.

warm potato and broad bean salad with tuna

10 small potatoes (1.2kg),
  sliced thickly
500g frozen broad beans
425g can tuna in springwater,
  drained, flaked
⅓ cup (80ml) bottled mustard
  dressing

preparation and cooking time
30 minutes
serves 4
nutritional count per serving
7.4g total fat (1.4g saturated fat);
1848kJ (442 cal); 50.9g carbohydrate;
34.6g protein; 15.3g fibre

1 Boil, steam or microwave potato and beans, separately, until tender; drain. When cool enough to handle, peel outer layer from beans.
2 Combine potato and beans in large bowl with tuna and dressing.

lamb and pesto focaccia

400g lamb fillets
¼ cup (65g) bottled basil pesto
20cm-square piece (60g)
  focaccia bread
½ cup (50g) thinly shaved
  parmesan cheese

preparation and cooking time
20 minutes
serves 2
nutritional count per serving
29.7g total fat (11.4g saturated fat);
2416kJ (578 cal); 19.6g carbohydrate;
57.5g protein; 1.9g fibre

1 Cook lamb in heated oiled large frying pan until cooked as desired. Cover lamb; stand 5 minutes then slice thickly.
2 Preheat sandwich press.
3 Cut bread in half lengthways then in half crossways. Spread pesto over two slices of bread, top with lamb, cheese and remaining bread.
4 Place focaccia in sandwich press; heat about 5 minutes or until cheese melts and focaccia is heated through. Slice diagonally to serve.

bean and tomato quesadillas

8 large flour tortillas (460g)
450g can refried beans
2 medium tomatoes (300g),
  chopped finely
2 cups (240g) coarsely grated
  cheddar cheese

preparation and cooking time
20 minutes
serves 4
nutritional count per serving
26.4g total fat (14g saturated fat);
2378kJ (569 cal); 49.7g carbohydrate;
28.8g protein; 8.9g fibre

1 Place one tortilla on board; spread with a quarter of the beans. Sprinkle with a quarter of the tomato and cheese. Top with second tortilla. Repeat with remaining tortillas, beans, tomato and cheese to make four quesadillas.
2 Cook quesadillas, one at a time, in heated oiled large frying pan, over medium heat, until browned lightly both sides. Cut into wedges; serve with sour cream, if you like.

chicken tandoori wrap

You will need one large barbecued chicken (900g) for this recipe.

3½ cups (600g) coarsely chopped cooked chicken

¼ cup (60g) tandoori paste

¾ cup (200g) yogurt

4 pieces lavash bread (240g)

preparation and cooking time
25 minutes

serves 4

nutritional count per serving
19.1g total fat (5.1g saturated fat);
2190kJ (524 cal); 39.7g carbohydrate;
46g protein; 3.5g fibre

1 Combine chicken, paste and ¼ cup of the yogurt in heated oiled medium frying pan; cook, stirring, about 5 minutes or until hot.

2 Place a quarter of the chicken mixture along short side of one piece of lavash; drizzle with a quarter of the remaining yogurt, roll to enclose filling. Repeat with remaining ingredients to make three more wraps. Serve with mango chutney, if desired.

lamb and rocket bruschetta

600g lamb backstraps (fillet)

½ loaf ciabatta bread (220g)

⅓ cup sun-dried tomato pesto

25g baby rocket leaves

preparation and cooking time
20 minutes

serves 4

nutritional count per serving
15g total fat (4.4g saturated fat);
1643kJ (393 cal); 25.8g carbohydrate;
37.6g protein; 2.2g fibre

1 Cook lamb in heated oiled medium frying pan until cooked as desired. Cover; stand 5 minutes then slice thinly.

2 Preheat grill.

3 Meanwhile, cut bread into eight slices; toast bread, both sides, under hot grill. Spread each slice with pesto. Divide sliced lamb among bruschetta; sprinkle with rocket leaves.

steak sandwich

3 beef eye-fillet steaks (450g)
2 small french bread sticks (300g)
40g trimmed watercress
1 tablespoon horseradish cream

preparation and cooking time
25 minutes
serves 4
nutritional count per serving
11g total fat (4.3g saturated fat);
1371kJ (328 cal); 20.7g carbohydrate;
35.3g protein; 1.7g fibre

1 Cook steaks in heated oiled medium frying pan until cooked as desired. Cover; stand 5 minutes then slice thinly.
2 Meanwhile, slice bread in half lengthways (do not cut all the way through), then cut each in half crossways. Fill each with equal amounts of watercress, beef and horseradish cream.

roast vegetable frittata

6 eggs
½ cup (125ml) cream
⅓ cup (40g) coarsely grated
  cheddar cheese
1½ cups coarsely chopped
  leftover roasted vegetables

preparation and cooking time
45 minutes
serves 4
nutritional count per serving
26.3g total fat (13.9g saturated fat);
1346kJ (322 cal); 6g carbohydrate;
15.1g protein; 2.1g fibre

1 Preheat oven to 180°C/160°C fan-forced. Oil 19cm-square cake pan; line base and sides with baking paper, extending paper 5cm above edges.
2 Whisk eggs, cream and cheese in large jug. Place vegetables in pan; pour egg mixture over vegetables.
3 Bake about 30 minutes or until frittata is set; stand in pan 10 minutes before cutting.

We used leftover roasted kumara, potato, red onion, zucchini and capsicum in this recipe, but any remaining roasted vegetables are suitable to use.

ham, egg and cheese toastie

2 slices wholemeal bread (90g)
30g shaved ham
1 hard-boiled egg, sliced thinly
¼ cup (30g) coarsely grated
reduced-fat cheddar cheese

1 Preheat sandwich press.
2 Sandwich ham, egg and cheese between bread slices.
3 Toast in sandwich press until golden brown. Serve with barbecue sauce, if desired.

preparation and cooking time
10 minutes
serves 1
nutritional count per serving
19.1g total fat (8.8g saturated fat);
1818kJ (435 cal); 34.3g carbohydrate;
28.6g protein; 5.7g fibre

spinach and corn pasties

2 medium potatoes (400g),
diced into 1cm pieces
250g frozen spinach,
thawed, drained
2 x 310g cans creamed corn
3 sheets ready-rolled
shortcrust pastry

1 Cook potato in heated oiled large frying pan, stirring, until browned lightly. Combine potato, spinach and corn in large bowl.
2 Preheat oven to 200°C/180°C fan-forced. Oil two oven trays.
3 Cut pastry sheets in half diagonally. Place equal amounts of filling on one half of each pastry triangle; fold pastry in half to enclose filling, press edges with fork to seal.
4 Place pasties on trays; spray with cooking-oil spray. Bake about 30 minutes or until browned lightly. Serve with sweet chilli sauce, if desired.

preparation and cooking time
1 hour
makes 6
nutritional count per pastie
23.7g total fat (12.1g saturated fat);
2140kJ (512 cal); 61.7g carbohydrate;
9.4g protein; 7.3g fibre

tip The quintessential easy Sunday night dinner, toasted sandwiches are both a comfort food and a satisfying meal wrapped into one. Using wholemeal or wholegrain bread and low-fat cheese also make them a healthy choice.

tip Originating from Cornwall in the United Kingdom, pasties were devised as a hearty meal for Cornish tin miners who couldn't come to the surface to eat. The traditional semi-circular shaped Cornish pasties were filled with diced meat, sliced potato and onion. Sometimes a sweet filling was added to one end of the pastie, making it a combined lunch and dessert meal in one.

honey, soy and sesame chicken wings

1kg chicken wings
¼ cup (60ml) japanese soy sauce
2 tablespoons honey
2 teaspoons sesame seeds

preparation and cooking time
45 minutes (plus refrigeration time)
serves 4
nutritional count per serving
8.4g total fat (2.7g saturated fat);
1145kJ (274 cal); 12.2g carbohydrate;
37g protein; 0.1g fibre

1 Cut chicken wings into three pieces at joints; discard tips. Combine sauce, honey and seeds in large bowl with chicken. Cover; refrigerate 3 hours or overnight.
2 Preheat oven to 220°C/200°C fan-forced.
3 Place chicken, in single layer, on oiled wire rack over large shallow baking dish; brush chicken with any remaining marinade. Roast about 30 minutes or until chicken is cooked.
4 Serve chicken wings sprinkled with sliced green onion, if desired.

green pea soup

1 small leek (200g), sliced thinly
2 large potatoes (600g),
    chopped coarsely
3 cups (360g) frozen peas
2 cups (500ml) vegetable stock

preparation and cooking time
30 minutes (plus cooling time)
serves 4
nutritional count per serving
8.2g total fat (0.3g saturated fat);
694kJ (166 cal); 24.3g carbohydrate;
10.3g protein; 8.2g fibre

1 Cook leek in heated oiled large frying pan, stirring, until leek softens. Add potato, peas, stock and 3 cups water; bring to the boil. Reduce heat; simmer, covered, about 10 minutes or until potato is tender. Cool 15 minutes.
2 Blend or process soup, in batches, until smooth. Return soup to same cleaned pan; stir over medium heat until hot.

potato and bacon patties

1kg potatoes, chopped coarsely
4 green onions, chopped finely
4 rindless bacon rashers (260g),
  chopped finely
½ cup (75g) plain flour

preparation and cooking time
45 minutes
serves 4
nutritional count per serving
9.8g total fat (3.5g saturated fat);
1463kJ (350 cal); 42.1g carbohydrate;
20.1g protein; 4.3g fibre

1 Boil, steam or microwave potato until tender; drain Mash potato in large bowl until smooth.
2 Meanwhile, cook onion and bacon in heated oiled large frying pan, stirring, until bacon is crisp. Add bacon mixture to potato; stir to combine.
3 Using floured hands, shape potato mixture into 12 patties. Roll patties in flour to coat; shake off excess.
4 Cook patties in heated oiled large frying pan, in batches, until browned lightly both sides.

spanish fried rice

You need to cook 1½ cups (300g)
white long-grain rice the day
before making this recipe.

2 chorizo sausages (340g),
  chopped coarsely
1 large red capsicum (350g),
  chopped finely
1 cup (160g) frozen corn kernels
3 cups cold cooked rice

preparation and cooking time
20 minutes
serves 4
nutritional count per serving
26.3g total fat (9.3g saturated fat);
278kJ (545 cal); 53.1g carbohydrate;
22.2g protein; 3.6g fibre

1 Cook chorizo and capsicum in heated oiled large frying pan, stirring, until chorizo is browned and crisp. Add corn; cook, stirring, 2 minutes.
2 Add rice; cook, stirring, until hot.

34

Sides

Freshly cooked vegetables and grains add colour and texture to your table. Often overlooked because the same dish is offered each time, these sides offer a delicious variety for each meal.

hash browns

1kg potatoes, unpeeled
1 small brown onion (80g),
   chopped finely
2 teaspoons finely chopped
   fresh rosemary
60g ghee

preparation and cooking time
40 minutes
makes 12
nutritional count per hash brown
5.1g total fat (3.3g saturated fat);
431kJ (103 cal); 11.3g carbohydrate;
2.1g protein; 1.8g fibre

1 Boil, steam or microwave potatoes until just tender; drain. Cool 10 minutes.
2 Peel potatoes; cut into 1cm cubes. Combine potato in large bowl with onion and rosemary.
3 Heat a third of the ghee in medium heavy-based frying pan; place four egg rings in pan. Spoon ¼ cup of the potato mixture into each egg ring; using spatula, spread mixture evenly to fill ring. Cook, pressing frequently with spatula, until browned; carefully turn each ring to brown other side. Drain on absorbent paper; cover to keep warm.
4 Repeat step 3 to make a total of 12 hash browns.

rösti

1kg potatoes
1 teaspoon salt
80g unsalted butter
2 tablespoons vegetable oil

preparation and cooking time
25 minutes
makes 8
nutritional count per rösti
13g total fat (6.1g saturated fat);
777kJ (186 cal); 14g carbohydrate;
2.6g protein; 1.7g fibre

1 Coarsely grate potatoes into large bowl; stir in salt, squeeze excess moisture from potatoes. Divide potato mixture into eight portions.
2 Heat 10g of the butter and 1 teaspoon of the oil in medium frying pan; spread one portion of the potato mixture over base of pan, flatten with spatula to form a firm pancake. Cook, uncovered, over medium heat, until golden brown on the underside; shake pan to loosen rösti, then invert onto large plate. Gently slide rösti back into pan; cook, uncovered, until other side is golden brown and potato is tender. Drain on absorbent paper; cover to keep warm.
3 Repeat step 2 to make a total of eight rösti.

tip Hash browns are a popular breakfast staple in the United States where they commonly dice or shred the potatoes before frying them. In the United Kingdom, leftover mashed potato is often used. Here, we've used sebago potatoes, which are identified by their smooth white skin and white flesh.

tip The Swiss created this potato pancake and it was originally a breakfast food favoured by farmers. Today, many Swiss people regard it as a national dish and it's a popular accompaniment to a meal. The Swiss also debate which kind of potato makes the best rösti. We've used russet burbank potatoes, which are large reddish-brown skinned potatoes with a white flesh.

the perfect mash

1kg potatoes, chopped coarsely
40g butter, softened
¾ cup (180ml) hot milk

preparation and cooking time
30 minutes
serves 4
nutritional count per serving
10.2g total fat (6.6g saturated fat);
1062kJ (254 cal); 31.7g carbohydrate;
7g protein; 3.6g fibre

1 Place potato in medium saucepan with enough cold water to barely cover potato. Boil, uncovered, over medium heat about 15 minutes or until potato is tender. Drain.
2 Using the back of a wooden spoon, push potato through fine sieve into large bowl. Stir butter and milk into potato; fold gently until mash is smooth and fluffy.

capsicum mash

2 medium capsicums (300g)
1kg potatoes, chopped coarsely
½ cup (125ml) hot milk
20g butter, softened

preparation and cooking time
35 minutes
serves 4
nutritional count per serving
5.7g total fat (3.5g saturated fat);
9.7kJ (217 cal); 31.9g carbohydrate;
7.2g protein; 4.1g fibre

1 Preheat oven to 250°C/230°C fan-forced.
2 Quarter capsicums; discard seeds and membranes. Roast capsicum, skin-side up, until skin blisters and blackens. Cover capsicum pieces with plastic or paper for 5 minutes then peel away skin; chop capsicum coarsely. Blend or process capsicum until smooth.
3 Meanwhile, boil, steam or microwave potato until tender; drain. Mash potato in large bowl; stir in milk and butter. Add capsicum to mash; stir until combined.

kumara mash

500g potatoes, chopped coarsely
500g kumara, peeled,
  chopped coarsely
¼ cup (60ml) hot chicken stock
40g butter, softened

1 Boil, steam or microwave potato and kumara, together, until tender; drain.
2 Mash potato and kumara in large bowl; stir in stock and butter.

preparation and cooking time
25 minutes
serves 4
nutritional count per serving
8.5g total fat (5.4g saturated fat);
932kJ (223 cal); 29.8g carbohydrate;
4.9g protein; 3.7g fibre

cumin pumpkin mash

500g potatoes, chopped coarsely
500g pumpkin, chopped coarsely
40g butter, softened
1 teaspoon ground cumin

1 Boil, steam or microwave potato and pumpkin, together, until tender; drain.
2 Mash potato and pumpkin in large bowl; stir in butter and cumin.

preparation and cooking time
30 minutes
serves 4
nutritional count per serving
8.7g total fat (5.7g saturated fat);
782kJ (187 cal); 20.9g carbohydrate;
4.8g protein; 3g fibre

baked potatoes

4 potatoes (1.5kg), unpeeled
1 teaspoon sea salt flakes
50g softened butter

preparation and cooking time
1 hour 10 minutes
serves 4
nutritional count per serving
10.6g total fat (6.8g saturated fat);
1371kJ (328 cal); 45.9g carbohydrate;
8.5g protein; 7g fibre

1 Preheat oven to 250°C/230°C fan-forced.
2 Pierce potato skins with a fork; wrap each potato in foil, place on oven tray. Bake about 1 hour or until tender.
3 Top with salt and butter, or use any of your favourite toppings.

scalloped potatoes

1.2kg potatoes
150g leg ham, chopped finely
600ml light cream
¾ cup (90g) coarsely grated
  cheddar cheese

preparation and cooking time
1 hour 20 minutes
serves 6
nutritional count per serving
49.4g total fat (32.1g saturated fat);
2521kJ (603 cal); 25.1g carbohydrate;
14.5g protein; 2.7g fibre

1 Preheat oven to 180°C/160°C fan-forced. Oil 1.5-litre (6-cup) baking dish.
2 Using sharp knife, mandoline or V-slicer, cut potatoes into very thin slices; pat dry with absorbent paper. Layer a quarter of the potato in prepared dish; top with a third of the ham. Continue layering remaining potato and ham, finishing with potato.
3 Heat cream in small saucepan until almost boiling; pour over potato mixture. Cover with foil; bake in oven 30 minutes. Remove foil; bake 20 minutes. Top with cheese; bake, uncovered, about 20 minutes or until potato is tender. Stand 10 minutes before serving.

hasselback potatoes

4 potatoes (800g),
   halved horizontally
2 tablespoons olive oil
¼ cup (25g) packaged breadcrumbs
½ cup (60g) finely grated
   cheddar cheese

preparation and cooking time
1 hour 20 minutes
serves 4
nutritional count per serving
14.6g total fat (4.6g saturated fat);
1158kJ (277 cal); 26.4g carbohydrate;
8.7g protein; 2.9g fibre

1 Preheat oven to 180°C/160°C fan-forced.
2 Place one potato half, cut-side down, on chopping board; place a chopstick along each side of potato. Slice potato thinly, cutting through to chopsticks to prevent cutting all the way through. Repeat with remaining potato.
3 Coat potato in half the oil in medium baking dish; place, rounded-side up, in a single layer. Roast, uncovered, 45 minutes, brushing with remaining oil. Continue roasting without brushing about 15 minutes or until potatoes are cooked through.
4 Sprinkle combined breadcrumbs and cheese over potatoes; roast, uncovered, 10 minutes or until topping is browned lightly.

sautéed potatoes

1kg potatoes, unpeeled
2 tablespoons olive oil
50g butter, chopped

preparation and cooking time
25 minutes
serves 4
nutritional count per serving
19.6g total fat (8g saturated fat);
1425kJ (341 cal); 32.8g carbohydrate;
6.1g protein; 5g fibre

1 Cut potatoes into 1cm-thick slices.
2 Heat oil and butter in large frying pan; cook potato, covered, over medium heat, turning occasionally, until browned lightly. Reduce heat; cook, tossing pan to turn potato, about 10 minutes or until tender.

potato skins with horseradish cream

1kg potatoes, unpeeled
¼ cup (60g) horseradish cream
¾ cup (180g) light sour cream
¼ teaspoon smoked paprika

preparation and cooking time
1 hour 15 minutes
serves 4
nutritional count per serving
10.7g total fat (6.8g saturated fat);
1200kJ (287 cal); 36.4g carbohydrate;
8g protein; 5.3g fibre

1 Preheat oven to 220°C/200°C fan-forced.
2 Scrub potatoes; spray with cooking-oil spray. Place potatoes on oven tray; bake, uncovered, about 50 minutes or until tender. Cool 10 minutes.
3 Cut each potato into six wedges; carefully remove flesh, leaving skins intact. Place potato skins, skin-side down, on wire rack over oven tray; spray with cooking-oil spray. Roast, uncovered, about 20 minutes or until crisp.
4 Meanwhile, combine horseradish cream, sour cream and paprika in small bowl.
5 Serve skins with horseradish cream.

cottage fries

1kg potatoes
30g butter, chopped
½ cup (125ml) vegetable oil
1 medium brown onion (150g), sliced thickly

preparation and cooking time
20 minutes (plus standing time)
serves 4
nutritional count per serving
35.1g total fat (7.7g saturated fat);
1935kJ (463 cal); 29.9g carbohydrate;
5.7g protein; 3.9g fibre

1 Using sharp knife, mandoline or V-slicer, slice potatoes into 2mm slices. Stand potato in large bowl of cold water 30 minutes. Drain; pat dry with absorbent paper.
2 Heat a third of the butter and a third of the oil in large frying pan; cook a third of the potato and a third of the onion, stirring occasionally, until browned lightly and cooked through. Drain on absorbent paper; cover to keep warm.
3 Repeat step 2, in two batches. Return cottage fries to pan; toss to heat through. Season with freshly cracked black pepper and sea salt, if you like.

pan-fried asparagus with parmesan

1 tablespoon olive oil
400g asparagus, trimmed
½ cup (40g) flaked
  parmesan cheese
½ teaspoon cracked black pepper

1 Heat oil in large frying pan; cook asparagus, in batches, until just tender.
2 Serve asparagus sprinkled with cheese and cracked pepper.

preparation and cooking time
10 minutes
serves 4
nutritional count per serving
7.9g total fat (2.7g saturated fat);
410kJ (98 cal); 1g carbohydrate;
5.5g protein; 1g fibre

mustard and honey-glazed roasted kumara

1kg kumara, unpeeled
⅓ cup (120g) honey
2 tablespoons wholegrain mustard
1 tablespoon coarsely chopped
  fresh rosemary

1 Preheat oven to 220°C/200°C fan-forced.
2 Halve kumara lengthways; cut each half into 2cm wedges.
3 Combine remaining ingredients in large bowl, add kumara; toss kumara to coat in mixture. Place kumara mixture in large shallow baking dish. Roast, uncovered, about 1 hour or until kumara is tender and slightly caramelised.

preparation and cooking time
1 hour 10 minutes
serves 4
nutritional count per serving
0.4g total fat (0g saturated fat);
1053kJ (252 cal); 54.9g carbohydrate;
4.5g protein; 4.1g fibre

tip A tasty and attractive side dish, these potato wedges are the perfect accompaniment to meat or fish, served with a crispy green salad.

tip Cafes and restaurants around the world use russet burbank potatoes to make their potato chips. These potatoes are large and, as the name suggests, they are russet (reddish brown) in colour with a white flesh. They are favoured for chip making because they create dark-coloured, caramelised chips.

potato wedges with lemon pepper

1kg potatoes, unpeeled
2 tablespoons olive oil
1 lemon
½ teaspoon freshly ground
  black pepper

preparation and cooking time
50 minutes
serves 4
nutritional count per serving
9.4g total fat (1.3g saturated fat);
1058kJ (253 cal); 33.2g carbohydrate;
6.1g protein; 5.1g fibre

1 Preheat oven to 220°C/200°C fan-forced.
Lightly oil two oven trays.
2 Scrub potatoes; cut into wedges. Toss wedges
and oil in large bowl. Place wedges, in single
layer, on oven trays; roast, uncovered, turning
occasionally, about 40 minutes or until crisp and
cooked through.
3 Meanwhile, grate rind from lemon (you need
3 teaspoons). Juice lemon (you need 1 tablespoon).
Combine rind, juice and pepper in small bowl.
4 Sprinkle lemon pepper all over wedges.

the perfect potato chip

1kg potatoes
peanut oil, for deep-frying

preparation and cooking time
30 minutes (plus standing time)
serves 4
nutritional count per serving
10.9g total fat (1.9g saturated fat);
986kJ (236 cal); 27.8g carbohydrate;
5.1g protein; 3.4g fibre

1 Cut potatoes lengthways into 1cm-thick
slices; cut each slice lengthways into 1cm-thick
chips. Stand potato in large bowl of cold water
30 minutes. Drain; pat dry with absorbent paper.
2 Heat oil in large saucepan; cook chips, in three
batches, about 4 minutes each batch or until just
tender but not browned. Drain on absorbent
paper; stand 10 minutes.
3 Reheat oil; cook chips, in three batches, until
crisp and golden brown. Drain on absorbent
paper. Serve chips sprinkled with sea salt, and
accompanied with tomato sauce, if you like.

potato scallops

300g potatoes
¾ cup (110g) self-raising flour
½ teaspoon sea salt flakes
peanut oil, for deep-frying

preparation and cooking time
35 minutes (plus standing time)
serves 6
nutritional count per serving
0.3g total fat (0g saturated fat);
410kJ (98 cal); 19.8g carbohydrate;
3g protein; 1.4g fibre

1 Using sharp knife, mandoline or V-slicer, cut potatoes into 2mm-thick slices. Stand potato in large bowl of cold water 30 minutes. Drain; pat dry with absorbent paper.
2 Meanwhile, place flour and salt in medium bowl; add 1 cup water, whisk until batter is smooth. Dip potato slices, one at a time, in batter.
3 Heat oil in large saucepan; deep-fry potato, in batches, until browned lightly and tender. Drain on absorbent paper.

balsamic-glazed baby onions

2 teaspoons balsamic vinegar
2 teaspoons wholegrain mustard
1 tablespoon honey
250g baby onions, halved

preparation and cooking time
25 minutes
serves 4
nutritional count per serving
0.2g total fat (0g saturated fat);
159kJ (38 cal); 7.8g carbohydrate;
0.9g protein; 0.6g fibre

1 Combine vinegar, mustard and honey in small saucepan; bring to the boil. Reduce heat; simmer, uncovered, about 2 minutes or until glaze thickens.
2 Cook onion in heated oiled large frying pan, brushing constantly with glaze, stirring, until browned and tender.

fresh peas, caraway and parmesan

60g butter
1 teaspoon caraway seeds
4 cups fresh peas (640g)
½ cup (40g) finely grated
    parmesan cheese

1 Melt butter in heated large frying pan; cook seeds, stirring, until fragrant.
2 Add peas to pan; cook, stirring, until peas are just tender. Serve peas sprinkled with cheese.

preparation and cooking time
25 minutes
serves 4
nutritional count per serving
16.2g total fat (10.2g saturated fat);
1158kJ (277 cal); 15.6g carbohydrate;
13.2g protein; 9g fibre

broccolini polonaise

60g butter, melted
½ cup (35g) stale breadcrumbs
2 hard-boiled eggs,
    chopped finely
350g broccolini

1 Heat half the butter in large frying pan; cook breadcrumbs, stirring, until browned and crisp. Combine breadcrumbs in small bowl with egg.
2 Boil, steam or microwave broccolini until just tender; drain.
3 Top broccolini with egg mixture then drizzle with remaining melted butter.

preparation and cooking time
20 minutes
serves 4
nutritional count per serving
15.7g total fat (9g saturated fat);
869kJ (208 cal); 6.5g carbohydrate;
8.8g protein; 3.9g fibre

baby carrots with orange maple syrup

800g baby carrots
1 large orange (300g)
25g butter
1 tablespoon maple syrup

preparation and cooking time
35 minutes
serves 4
nutritional count per serving
5.3g total fat (3.4g saturated fat);
502kJ (120 cal); 14.2g carbohydrate;
1.5g protein; 5.1g fibre

1 Boil, steam or microwave carrots until just tender.
2 Meanwhile, grate rind from orange (you need 1 teaspoon). Juice orange (you need 1 tablespoon.)
3 Melt butter in heated large frying pan, add rind, juice and syrup; cook, stirring, until mixture boils. Reduce heat; simmer, uncovered, until syrup mixture thickens slightly. Add drained carrots to pan; stir gently to coat in orange maple syrup.

baby beetroot with caper vinaigrette

500g baby beetroot
2 teaspoons rinsed, drained baby capers
1 tablespoon white wine vinegar
1 tablespoon olive oil

preparation and cooking time
30 minutes
serves 4
nutritional count per serving
4.7g total fat (0.6g saturated fat);
272kJ (95 cal); 9.4g carbohydrate;
2.1g protein; 3.4g fibre

1 Trim stems from beetroot, leaving a 2cm length; cook beetroot in large saucepan of boiling water, uncovered, about 20 minutes or until tender. Drain; cool 10 minutes. Peel beetroot.
2 Place beetroot in large bowl with remaining ingredients; toss gently to combine.

gai lan in oyster sauce

1kg gai lan
1 tablespoon peanut oil
1 tablespoon japanese soy sauce
2 tablespoons oyster sauce

1 Boil, steam or microwave gai lan until just tender; drain.
2 Heat oil in wok; stir-fry gai lan and sauces about 2 minutes or until gai lan is tender.

preparation and cooking time
10 minutes
serves 4
nutritional count per serving
5.2g total fat (0.8g saturated fat);
364kJ (87 cal); 5.2g carbohydrate;
3.4g protein; 3.3g fibre

creamed mint peas

500g frozen peas
2 cloves garlic, unpeeled
½ cup (140g) low-fat yogurt
½ cup fresh mint leaves

1 Cook peas and garlic in saucepan of boiling water until peas soften; drain.
2 Peel garlic; blend or process garlic, peas, yogurt and mint until smooth.

preparation and cooking time
15 minutes
serves 4
nutritional count per serving
0.7g total fat (0.1g saturated fat);
410kJ (98 cal); 9.6g carbohydrate;
9.5g protein; 8g fibre

sesame patty-pan **squash** and sugar snap peas

8 yellow patty-pan squash (240g)
150g sugar snap peas, trimmed
2 teaspoons japanese soy sauce
2 teaspoons toasted sesame seeds

1 Boil, steam or microwave squash and peas, separately, until tender; drain.
2 Place vegetables in large bowl with remaining ingredients; toss gently to combine.

preparation and cooking time
15 minutes
serves 4
nutritional count per serving
1g total fat (0.1g saturated fat); 184kJ (44 cal); 4g carbohydrate; 3.6g protein; 2.4g fibre

green **beans** almondine

300g green beans
20g butter
2 rindless bacon rashes (130g), chopped finely
¼ cup (25g) slivered almonds

1 Boil, steam or microwave beans until just tender; drain. Rinse under cold water; drain.
2 Melt butter in heated large frying pan; cook bacon and nuts, stirring, until bacon is crisp. Add beans; stir until hot.

preparation and cooking time
15 minutes
serves 4
nutritional count per serving
11.5g total fat (3.9g saturated fat); 602kJ (144 cal); 2.3g carbohydrate; 6.9g protein; 2.9g fibre

tip Sugar snap peas are very similar to snow peas, but they have rounder pods. As the name suggests, sugar snap peas are sweet, crunchy and juicy. They liven up the dinner plate.

tip For a vegetarian option on this recipe, you could substitute cubed tofu, tempeh (soy bean meal) or eggplant for the bacon.

parmesan and baby spinach salad

150g baby spinach leaves
50g shaved parmesan cheese
1 tablespoon roasted pine nuts
¼ cup (60ml) bottled balsamic
   dressing

1 Place spinach leaves, cheese and nuts in large bowl.
2 Drizzle dressing over salad; toss gently to combine.

preparation time 10 minutes
serves 4
nutritional count per serving
6.7g total fat (2.7g saturated fat);
368kJ (88 cal); 0.4g carbohydrate;
6.1g protein; 1.2g fibre

barbecued corn, broad beans and capsicum

2 trimmed corn cobs (500g)
250g frozen broad beans,
   thawed, peeled
1 small red capsicum (150g),
   chopped finely
10g butter

1 Cook corn on heated oiled grill plate (or grill or barbecue) until just tender. When cool enough to handle, use sharp knife to cut kernels from cobs.
2 Meanwhile, boil, steam or microwave broad beans until tender; drain.
3 Place corn and beans in large bowl with capsicum and butter; toss gently to combine.

preparation and cooking time
30 minutes
serves 4
nutritional count per serving
3.4g total fat (1.4g saturated fat);
681kJ (163 cal); 21g carbohydrate;
7.4g protein; 9.2g fibre

cheesy polenta

2⅓ cups (580ml) milk
1 cup (170g) polenta
½ cup (70g) finely grated
   parmesan cheese
30g butter

1 Combine milk with 2⅓ cups water in large saucepan; bring to the boil. Gradually add polenta to liquid, stirring constantly. Reduce heat; simmer, stirring, about 10 minutes or until polenta thickens. Stir in cheese and butter.

preparation and cooking time
20 minutes
serves 4
nutritional count per serving
18.2g total fat (11.4g saturated fat);
1547kJ (370 cal); 36.1g carbohydrate;
14.9g protein; 1.2g fibre

pilaf

1 clove garlic, crushed
1 cup (200g) basmati rice
¼ cup coarsely chopped fresh
   flat-leaf parsley
¼ cup (40g) toasted
   flaked almonds

1 Cook garlic in heated oiled medium saucepan, stirring, until fragrant. Add rice; cook, stirring, 1 minute. Add 2 cups water; bring to the boil.
2 Reduce heat; simmer, covered, about 20 minutes or until rice is just tender. Remove from heat; fluff rice with fork. Stir in parsley and almonds.

preparation and cooking time
30 minutes
serves 4
nutritional count per serving
5.9g total fat (1.4g saturated fat);
999kJ (239 cal); 40g carbohydrate;
5.5g protein; 1.6g fibre

steamed lemon jasmine rice

1 cup (200g) jasmine rice
1½ cups (375ml) chicken stock
2 teaspoons finely grated
  lemon rind
¼ cup finely chopped fresh chives

preparation and cooking time
25 minutes
serves 4
nutritional count per serving
0.7g total fat (0.2g saturated fat);
803kJ (192 cal); 41.2g carbohydrate;
4.5g protein; 0.5g fibre

1 Combine rice, stock and ½ cup water in large saucepan; bring to the boil. Reduce heat; simmer, covered tightly, about 10 minutes or until rice is cooked.
2 Remove from heat; stand, covered, 5 minutes. Stir in rind and chives.

spinach couscous

1½ cups (300g) couscous
20g butter
80g baby spinach leaves,
  sliced thinly

preparation time 10 minutes
serves 4
nutritional count per serving
4.6g total fat (2.8g saturated fat);
1329kJ (318 cal); 57.6g carbohydrate;
10.1g protein; 1.2g fibre

1 Combine couscous with 1½ cups boiling water in large heatproof bowl, cover; stand about 5 minutes or until liquid is absorbed, fluffing with fork occasionally.
2 Stir butter and spinach into couscous.

yellow coconut rice

1¾ cups (350g) white
  long-grain rice
400ml can coconut cream
½ teaspoon ground turmeric
pinch saffron threads

preparation and cooking time
20 minutes (plus standing time)
serves 4
nutritional count per serving
21.7g total fat (18.7g saturated fat);
2190kJ (524 cal); 73g carbohydrate;
7.8g protein; 2.5g fibre

1 Stand rice in large bowl of cold water
30 minutes. Drain rice; rinse under cold water
until water runs clear. Drain.
2 Place rice and remaining ingredients with
1¼ cups water in large heavy-based saucepan;
cover, bring to the boil, stirring occasionally.
Reduce heat; simmer, covered, about 15 minutes
or until rice is tender. Remove from heat; stand,
covered, 5 minutes before serving.

date and pine nut couscous

2 cups (400g) couscous
8 dried dates, sliced thinly
½ cup (80g) roasted pine nuts
2 tablespoons coarsely chopped
  fresh coriander

preparation time 10 minutes
serves 4
nutritional count per serving
14.6g total fat (0.9g saturated fat);
2261kJ (541 cal); 84.3g carbohydrate;
15.7g protein; 2.9g fibre

1 Combine couscous with 2 cups boiling water
in large heatproof bowl, cover; stand about
5 minutes or until liquid is absorbed, fluffing
with fork occasionally.
2 Stir dates, nuts and coriander into couscous.

34

Sauces + Dressings

When your meal involves dipping, drizzling and pouring, it adds a creative dimension to your eating experience and enhances all the flavours on the plate.

beurre blanc

¼ cup (60ml) dry white wine
1 tablespoon lemon juice
¼ cup (60ml) cream
125g cold butter, chopped

preparation and cooking time
20 minutes
makes 1 cup
nutritional count per tablespoon
10.4g total fat (6.8g saturated fat);
406kJ (97 cal); 0.3g carbohydrate;
0.2g protein; 0g fibre
Sauce goes well with grilled salmon
or trout fillets.

1 Combine wine and juice in small saucepan;
bring to the boil. Boil, without stirring, until
reduced by two-thirds. Add cream; return to the
boil then reduce heat. Whisk in cold butter, piece
by piece, whisking between additions, until sauce
is smooth and thickened slightly.

hollandaise

2 tablespoons white vinegar
¼ teaspoon cracked black pepper
2 egg yolks
200g unsalted butter, melted

preparation and cooking time
25 minutes
makes 1 cup
nutritional count per tablespoon
14.5g total fat (9.2g saturated fat);
548kJ (131 cal); 0.1g carbohydrate;
0.5g protein; 0g fibre
Sauce goes well with poached eggs,
steamed asparagus and grilled fish.

1 Combine vinegar, pepper and 2 tablespoons
water in small saucepan; bring to the boil. Reduce
heat; simmer, uncovered, until liquid reduces to
1 tablespoon. Strain through fine sieve into
medium heatproof bowl; cool 10 minutes.
2 Whisk egg yolks into vinegar mixture until
combined. Set bowl over medium saucepan
of simmering water (do not allow water to
touch base of bowl). Whisk over heat until
mixture is thickened.
3 Remove bowl from heat; gradually add melted
butter in a thin, steady stream, whisking
constantly until sauce has thickened.

tip A classic French butter sauce, buerre blanc originates in the Loire Valley. It is traditionally made with a reduction of vinegar or white wine, shallots and cold butter (not cream), but there are endless contemporary versions. The cream helps to make the sauce smooth and thick, but its inclusion is debated by followers of the original French method.

tip Care and patience are needed to bring this sauce into being: follow the directions to the letter and ensure you don't overcook it. The texture needs to be smooth and creamy, and the flavour rich and buttery. The care you give it will be worthwhile.

pumpkin and sage sauce

1 tablespoon olive oil
8 large fresh sage leaves
500g pumpkin, cut into 1cm cubes
¾ cup (180ml) cream

preparation and cooking time
35 minutes
makes 2 cups
nutritional count per tablespoon
24.4g total fat (13.8g saturated fat);
1095kJ (262 cal); 7.8g carbohydrate;
3g protein; 1.2g fibre
Sauce goes well with grilled pork
and chicken, and with pasta such
as fettuccine or ravioli.

1 Heat oil in large frying pan; cook sage, stirring
gently, until bright green and crisp. Drain on
absorbent paper.
2 Cook pumpkin in same pan, uncovered, stirring
occasionally, about 15 minutes or until browned
lightly and just tender.
3 Meanwhile, bring cream to the boil in medium
saucepan. Reduce heat; simmer, uncovered,
5 minutes. Add cream to pumpkin in pan; stir
over low heat until sauce is heated through.
Stir in sage leaves.

spinach cream sauce

1 medium brown onion (150g),
   chopped finely
½ cup (125ml) dry white wine
1 cup (250ml) cream
300g baby spinach leaves,
   shredded coarsely

preparation and cooking time
15 minutes
makes 2 cups
nutritional count per tablespoon
4.5g total fat (3g saturated fat);
209kJ (50 cal); 0.7g carbohydrate;
0.6g protein; 0.4g fibre
Sauce goes well with grilled
chicken and fish.

1 Cook onion in heated oiled large frying pan
until soft. Stir in wine and cream; bring to
the boil. Boil, uncovered, 2 minutes or until
thickened slightly.
2 Add spinach to pan; cook, stirring, until
spinach is just wilted.

fennel and pernod sauce

2 medium fennel bulbs (600g)
40g butter
⅓ cup (80ml) pernod
300ml cream

preparation and cooking time
30 minutes
makes 2 cups
nutritional count per tablespoon
6.8g total fat (4.5g saturated fat);
339kJ (81 cal); 2.4g carbohydrate;
0.4g protein; 0.4g fibre
Sauce goes well with grilled
scallops, prawns and fish.

1 Cut fronds from fennel; chop finely. Slice fennel thinly.
2 Melt butter in heated large frying pan; cook fennel, stirring occasionally, about 20 minutes or until softened. Add pernod and cream; bring to the boil. Simmer, uncovered, about 3 minutes or until thickened slightly. Stir in fennel fronds.

béchamel sauce

30g butter
2 tablespoons plain flour
1¼ cups (310ml) hot milk
pinch nutmeg

preparation and cooking time
20 minutes
makes 1 cup
nutritional count per tablespoon
3.1g total fat (2.1g saturated fat);
176kJ (42 cal); 2.6g carbohydrate;
1.1g protein; 0.1g fibre
Sauce goes well with grilled fish
fillets and with pasta dishes such
as pastichio or lasagne.

1 Melt butter in heated medium saucepan, add flour; cook, stirring, until mixture bubbles and thickens. Gradually add milk, stirring, until mixture boils and thickens. Stir nutmeg into sauce.

mornay sauce

1 cup (250ml) bottled
  béchamel sauce
¼ cup (60ml) cream
1 egg yolk
1 cup (120g) coarsely grated
  emmentaler cheese

1 Bring sauce to the boil in medium saucepan; add cream and egg yolk, whisk 1 minute.

2 Remove sauce from heat; add cheese, stir until cheese melts.

preparation and cooking time
10 minutes
makes 2 cups
nutritional count per tablespoon
4.4g total fat (2.8g saturated fat);
222kJ (53 cal); 1.4g carbohydrate;
2.2g protein; 0g fibre
Sauce goes well with cauliflower,
broccoli and grilled or steamed fish.

seafood sauce

¾ cup (180ml) dry white wine
1½ cups (375ml) bottled
  béchamel sauce
250g marinara mix, drained
2 tablespoons finely chopped
  fresh dill

1 Bring wine to the boil in medium frying pan. Reduce heat; simmer, uncovered, until liquid is reduced by half.

2 Add sauce and marinara mix to pan; bring to the boil. Reduce heat; simmer, uncovered, about 5 minutes or until seafood is cooked through. Stir in dill.

preparation and cooking time
25 minutes
makes 2 cups
nutritional count per ½ cup
11.2g total fat (6.6g saturated fat);
103kJ (240 cal); 8.7g carbohydrate;
18.8g protein; 0.3g fibre
Sauce goes well with grilled fish
fillets, pasta and grilled beef fillets.

chicken veloute

2¼ cups (560ml) chicken stock
40g butter
2 tablespoons plain flour

preparation and cooking time
35 minutes
makes 1½ cups
nutritional count per tablespoon
2g total fat (1.3g saturated fat);
100kJ (24 cal); 1.1g carbohydrate;
0.5g protein; 0.1g fibre
Sauce goes well with grilled chicken
breast fillets and pork cutlets.

1 Place stock in small saucepan; bring to the boil then remove from heat.
2 Melt butter in medium saucepan, add flour; cook, stirring, about 2 minutes or until mixture bubbles and thickens. Gradually stir hot stock into flour mixture; bring to the boil. Cook, stirring, until sauce boils and thickens.
3 Reduce heat; simmer, uncovered, about 20 minutes or until reduced by half. Strain sauce into small bowl.

warm dill and lemon sauce

⅓ cup (80ml) olive oil
2 teaspoons finely grated
   lemon rind
¼ cup lemon juice
2 tablespoons finely chopped
   fresh dill

preparation and cooking time
10 minutes
makes ½ cup
nutritional count per tablespoon
12.2g total fat (1.7g saturated fat);
456kJ (109 cal); 0.3g carbohydrate;
0.1g protein; 0.1g fibre
Sauce goes well with grilled squid,
poached salmon, pan-fried chicken
and duck breasts.

1 Heat oil in small saucepan until just warm. Remove from heat.
2 Stir in remaining ingredients.

chilli sauce

10 fresh long red chillies,
  chopped coarsely
1 tablespoon white vinegar
1 tablespoon caster sugar

preparation and cooking time
20 minutes
makes 1¼ cups
nutritional count per tablespoon
0g total fat (0g saturated fat);
21kJ (5 cal); 1.3g carbohydrate;
0g protein; 0g fibre
Sauce goes well with roasted
chicken wings, potato wedges
and chicken schnitzel.

1 Place chilli and 1¼ cups water in small
saucepan; bring to the boil. Reduce heat;
simmer, uncovered, 15 minutes.
2 Stir in vinegar and sugar. Blend or
process until smooth.

hoisin and peanut dipping sauce

1 tablespoon caster sugar
2 tablespoons rice vinegar
½ cup (125ml) hoisin sauce
2 tablespoons crushed unsalted
  peanuts, roasted

preparation and cooking time
5 minutes
makes 1 cup
nutritional count per tablespoon
1.5g total fat (0.2g saturated fat);
171kJ (41 cal); 5.7g carbohydrate;
0.7g protein; 1.3g fibre
Sauce goes well with grilled pork
cutlets, pork spareribs, and as a
marinade for chicken wings.

1 Combine sugar, vinegar and ½ cup water in
small saucepan; stir over heat until sugar dissolves.
2 Add sauce; bring to the boil. Reduce heat;
simmer, uncovered, about 5 minutes or until
thickened slightly. Remove from heat; stir in nuts.

cucumber raita

¼ teaspoon black mustard seeds
¼ teaspoon cumin seeds
2 lebanese cucumbers (260g),
  seeded, chopped finely
500g yogurt

1 Cook seeds in heated oiled small frying pan, stirring, over low heat, about 2 minutes or until seeds pop.
2 Combine seeds and remaining ingredients in medium bowl; mix well.

preparation and cooking time
10 minutes
serves 6
nutritional count per serving
3g total fat (1.9g saturated fat);
263kJ (63 cal); 4.7g carbohydrate;
4.2g protein; 0.4g fibre
Raita goes well with curries, spiced roast lamb and tandoori chicken.

spinach raita

500g spinach
¾ cup (210g) yogurt
1 teaspoon lemon juice
½ teaspoon ground cumin

1 Boil, steam or microwave spinach until just wilted; drain. When cool enough to handle, squeeze excess liquid from spinach.
2 Blend or process spinach with remaining ingredients until smooth.

preparation and cooking time
10 minutes
serves 4
nutritional count per serving
2.2g total fat (1.2g saturated fat);
255kJ (61 cal); 3.3g carbohydrate;
5.5g protein; 3.4g fibre
Raita goes well with curries, spiced roasted chicken and onion fritters.

tip Aromatic and sweet-tasting, mint is an ingredient used in cooking around the globe. It also has medicinal properties as a mild decongestant and an aid to digestion. Mint is very easy to grow, it tolerates a wide range of conditions and the leaves can be picked year-round.

tip This tart, citrus-based sauce is one of the mainstays of Japanese cuisine. In Japan, ponzu sauce is usually made with a citrus fruit called yuzu, which is not easy to obtain outside Asia. It is served with dishes such as sashimi and tempura.

mint sauce

2 cups firmly packed fresh
  mint leaves
3/4 cup (180ml) white wine vinegar
2 tablespoons caster sugar

preparation and cooking time
10 minutes (plus standing time)
makes 1 cup
nutritional count per tablespoon
0.1g total fat (0g saturated fat);
67kJ (16 cal); 3.2g carbohydrate;
0.3g protein; 0.6g fibre
Sauce goes well with roast lamb,
crumbed lamb cutlets, felafel and
a mixed bean or rice salad.

1 Chop half the mint coarsely; place in small
heatproof bowl.
2 Combine vinegar, sugar and 1/4 cup water in
small saucepan; stir over heat, without boiling,
until sugar dissolves. Pour liquid over chopped
mint, cover; stand 3 hours.
3 Strain liquid into bowl; discard mint. Chop
remaining mint coarsely; stir into liquid. Blend
or process until chopped finely.

ponzu sauce

1/4 cup (60ml) lemon juice
1/4 cup (60ml) tamari
2 green onions, sliced thinly

preparation time 10 minutes
makes 1 cup
nutritional count per tablespoon
0g total fat (0g saturated fat);
17kJ (4 cal); 0.3g carbohydrate;
0.4g protein; 0g fibre
Sauce goes well with baked whole
baby snapper, steamed white fish
fillets, steamed asian greens and
stir-fried tofu.
If tamari is not available, use
japanese soy sauce, instead.

1 Combine ingredients with 1/4 cup water in
small bowl.

carrot raita

5 fresh curry leaves,
    chopped finely
1 teaspoon black mustard seeds
2 medium carrots (240g),
    grated coarsely
250g yogurt

1 Cook leaves and seeds in heated oiled small frying pan, stirring, over low heat, 2 minutes or until seeds pop.
2 Combine leaves, seeds and remaining ingredients in medium bowl; mix well.

preparation and cooking time
10 minutes
serves 6
nutritional count per serving
4.4g total fat (2g saturated fat);
347kJ (83 cal); 6.1g carbohydrate;
4.2g protein; 1.2g fibre
Raita goes well with curries,
vegetable samosas and pea pakoras.

mayonnaise

2 egg yolks
3/4 teaspoon mustard powder
1 cup (250ml) extra light olive oil
1 tablespoon white vinegar

1 Combine egg yolks and mustard in medium bowl. Gradually add oil in a thin, steady stream, whisking constantly until mixture thickens. Stir in vinegar.

preparation time 15 minutes
makes 1 cup
nutritional count per tablespoon
19.1g total fat (2.8g saturated fat);
715kJ (171 cal); 0g carbohydrate;
0.5g protein; 0g fibre
Dressing goes well with cold meats
and vegetables, as a sandwich filling,
salad dressing or dipping sauce.

aïoli

4 cloves garlic, quartered
1 teaspoon sea salt
2 teaspoons lemon juice
1 cup (250ml) bottled mayonnaise

1 Using mortar and pestle, crush garlic and salt to a smooth paste.
2 Combine garlic mixture and remaining ingredients in small bowl.

preparation time 20 minutes
makes 1 cup
nutritional count per tablespoon
19.1g total fat (2.8g saturated fat);
719kJ (172 cal); 0.2g carbohydrate;
0.6g protein; 0.2g fibre
Aïoli goes well with grilled white fish fillets, crudités, and fried or boiled potatoes.

cranberry and raspberry vinaigrette

¼ cup (60ml) red wine vinegar
½ cup (125ml) olive oil
150g fresh raspberries
¼ cup (80g) whole-berry
   cranberry sauce

1 Blend or process ingredients until smooth. Push dressing through fine sieve into small bowl.

preparation time 5 minutes
makes 1 cup
nutritional count per tablespoon
9.5g total fat (1.3g saturated fat);
418kJ (100 cal); 3.4g carbohydrate;
0.2g protein; 0.7g fibre
Vinaigrette goes well with radicchio salad, grilled goats cheese salad and crumbed camembert.

pesto crème fraîche

200ml crème fraîche
2 tablespoons bottled basil pesto
2 tablespoons finely grated
   parmesan cheese
1 tablespoon lemon juice

1 Combine ingredients in small bowl; cover, refrigerate until cold.

preparation time 5 minutes
(plus refrigeration time)
makes 1 cup
nutritional count per tablespoon
10.3g total fat (4.9g saturated fat);
414kJ (99 cal); 0.6g carbohydrate;
1.2g protein; 0.2g fibre
Sauce goes well with roasted
potato wedges, grilled chicken
breasts, roasted vegetables and
as a potato salad dressing.

sesame soy dressing

1 tablespoon toasted
   sesame seeds
1 tablespoon sesame oil
2 tablespoons kecap manis
¼ cup (60ml) lime juice

1 Combine ingredients in small bowl.

preparation time 5 minutes
makes ½ cup
nutritional count per tablespoon
0.6g total fat (0.2g saturated fat);
71kJ (17 cal); 2.3g carbohydrate;
0.3g protein; 0g fibre
Dressing goes well with crudités
and steamed vegetables.

russian dressing

1 large beetroot (200g),
  unpeeled, trimmed
2 tablespoons coarsely chopped
  pickled onions
1 tablespoon rinsed, drained capers
½ cup (120g) sour cream

1 Cook beetroot in medium saucepan of boiling
water until tender; drain, reserving ¼ cup of the
cooking liquid. When cool enough to handle,
peel then chop beetroot coarsely.
2 Blend or process beetroot with remaining
ingredients and reserved liquid until smooth.

preparation and cooking time
25 minutes
makes 1½ cups
nutritional count per tablespoon
14g total fat (9.2g saturated fat);
681kJ (163 cal); 7g carbohydrate;
1.8g protein; 1.8g fibre
Dressing goes well with salad greens,
crudités, roast beef or veal, in a cold
pasta salad with cucumber, caper
and red onion.

french dressing

⅓ cup (80ml) white wine vinegar
2 teaspoons dijon mustard
½ teaspoon white sugar
⅔ cup (160ml) olive oil

1 Combine vinegar, mustard and sugar in
small bowl.
2 Gradually add oil in a thin, steady stream,
whisking constantly until mixture thickens.

preparation time 5 minutes
makes 1 cup
nutritional count per tablespoon
12.2g total fat (1.7g saturated fat);
456kJ (109 cal); 0.2g carbohydrate;
0g protein; 0g fibre
Dressing goes well with any type
of salad or salad greens.

choc marshmallow sauce

4 x 60g Mars Bars, chopped finely
300ml cream
100g packet marshmallows

1 Stir chocolate bars and cream in small saucepan, over low heat, until smooth. Add marshmallows, stir until smooth.

preparation and cooking time
20 minutes
makes 2 cups
nutritional count per tablespoon
7.2g total fat (4.6g saturated fat);
460kJ (116 cal); 10.3g carbohydrate;
0.9g protein; 0.2g fibre
Sauce goes well with chocolate cake, apple pie, as a fondue with fruit and over ice-cream.

sabayon

3 egg yolks
¼ cup (55g) caster sugar
¼ cup (60ml) dry white wine

1 Combine ingredients in medium bowl set over medium saucepan of simmering water (do not allow water to touch base of bowl). Whisk vigorously and continually about 5 minutes or until sauce is thick and creamy.

preparation and cooking time
10 minutes
makes 2 cups
nutritional count per tablespoon
0.7g total fat (0.2g saturated fat);
79kJ (19 cal); 2.3g carbohydrate;
0.4g protein; 0g fibre
Sauce goes well with grilled peaches or nectarines, poached pears and fresh mango slices.

strawberry coulis

300g frozen strawberries, thawed
1 tablespoon icing sugar

preparation time 10 minutes
makes 1 cup
nutritional count per tablespoon
0.3g total fat (0g saturated fat);
42kJ (10 cal); 1.6g carbohydrate;
0.4g protein; 0.6g fibre
Sauce goes well with puddings,
slices and poached fruits.

1 Push berries through fine sieve into small bowl; discard seeds. Stir in sifted icing sugar until combined.

rich caramel sauce

1 cup (220g) caster sugar
300ml thickened cream

preparation and cooking time
25 minutes
makes 1½ cups
nutritional count per tablespoon
6.2g total fat (4.1g saturated fat);
451kJ (108 cal); 12.7g carbohydrate;
0.4g protein; 0g fibre
Sauce goes well with apple pie,
grilled bananas, apple teacake and
sticky date pudding.

1 Combine sugar and ½ cup water in small saucepan; stir over low heat until sugar dissolves. Bring to the boil; boil, uncovered, without stirring, about 15 minutes or until mixture turns a caramel colour.
2 Remove from heat; allow bubbles to subside. Gradually add cream to caramel mixture; return to heat. Cook over low heat, stirring constantly, until sauce is smooth. Cool 10 minutes.

fudge sauce

200g dark eating chocolate
20g butter
¼ teaspoon vanilla extract
½ cup (125ml) cream

preparation and cooking time
15 minutes
makes 1 cup
nutritional count per tablespoon
10.6g total fat (6.7g saturated fat);
585kJ (140 cal); 10.7g carbohydrate;
1.1g protein; 0.2g fibre
Sauce goes well with ice-cream,
puddings, mousse and poached fruit.

1 Place chocolate and butter in small heatproof bowl set over small saucepan of simmering water (do not allow water to touch base of bowl). Stir until chocolate is melted. Add extract and cream; stir until combined. Serve sauce warm.

crème anglaise

1 vanilla bean, halved lengthways
1½ cups (375ml) milk
⅓ cup (75g) caster sugar
4 egg yolks

preparation and cooking time
30 minutes (plus refrigeration time)
makes 1½ cups
nutritional count per tablespoon
2.1g total fat (0.9g saturated fat);
184kJ (44 cal); 5.2g carbohydrate;
1.4g protein; 0g fibre
Sauce goes well with apple pie,
poached plums, chocolate cake
and fresh figs.

1 Scrape vanilla bean seeds into medium saucepan; add pod, milk and one tablespoon of the sugar. Bring to the boil then strain into large jug. Discard pod.
2 Meanwhile, combine egg yolks and remaining sugar in medium heatproof bowl set over medium saucepan of simmering water (do not allow water to touch base of bowl). Whisk until mixture is thick and creamy then gradually whisk in the hot milk mixture.
3 Return custard mixture to pan; stir over low heat until mixture is just thick enough to coat the back of a spoon.
4 Return custard to bowl; refrigerate about 1 hour or until cold.

tip Recent studies have shown that eating good quality dark chocolate (with a high cocoa content) can actually be good for you. Cocoa contains antioxidants that can help lower blood pressure, help prevent heart disease and improve digestion. But it must be top quality dark chocolate and eaten in moderation.

tip You can buy vanilla beans from gourmet grocers, selected health-food stores and most large supermarkets. It's more time consuming to use the bean rather than the extract, but it gives a fuller vanilla flavour.

34

Desserts

Some think it's the most important part of the meal, and these recipes prove you don't need a long list of ingredients or hours of preparation to create sweet and sumptuous desserts.

white chocolate and black cherry creamed rice

1.5 litres (6 cups) milk
2/3 cup (130g) arborio rice
120g white eating chocolate,
  chopped finely
425g can seedless black cherries,
  drained

preparation and cooking time
55 minutes
serves 6
nutritional count per serving
16.6g total fat (10.6g saturated fat);
1593kJ 381 cal); 45.6g carbohydrate;
11.7g protein; 0.8g fibre

1 Combine milk, rice and half the chocolate in medium saucepan; bring to the boil. Reduce heat; simmer over very low heat, stirring often, about 40 minutes or until rice is tender.
2 Serve rice warm, topped with cherries and remaining chocolate. Sprinkle with nutmeg, if desired.

apple and blackberry jellies

85g packet blackcurrant
  jelly crystals
1 cup (150g) frozen blackberries
1 medium apple (150g), peeled,
  cored, chopped finely
1/2 cup (125ml) thickened cream

preparation and cooking time
10 minutes (plus refrigeration time)
serves 4
nutritional count per serving
11.8g total fat (7.6g saturated fat);
957kJ (229 cal); 26.7g carbohydrate;
2.8g protein; 2.8g fibre

1 Make jelly according to directions on packet.
2 Divide blackberries and apple among four 3/4-cup (180ml) glasses; pour jelly over top. Refrigerate about 3 hours or until jelly has set.
3 Beat cream in small bowl with electric mixer until soft peaks form. Serve jellies topped with whipped cream.

tip Cooking the milk, rice and white chocolate together gives this dessert a luxurious, velvety texture that is perfectly offset by the sweet tanginess of the black cherries.

tip These jellies are so simple to make, and yet they create such an impressive-looking dessert, especially when served in sophisticated glassware. Make them ahead of time and take the stress out of your dinner party.

choc-cherry mascarpone

425g can sour cherries in syrup
300ml thickened cream
200g dark eating chocolate,
  chopped coarsely
250g mascarpone cheese

preparation and cooking time
15 minutes (plus cooling and
refrigeration time)
serves 6
nutritional count per serving
52g total fat (33.6g saturated fat);
2475kJ (592 cal); 28.6g carbohydrate;
3.6g protein; 1g fibre

1 Drain cherries, reserve ¼ cup of syrup.
2 Combine cream and reserved syrup in medium
saucepan; bring to the boil. Remove from heat;
add chocolate, stir until smooth. Cool.
3 Beat cheese and chocolate mixture in small
bowl with electric mixer until smooth.
4 Divide cherries between six ¾-cup (180ml)
dishes; top with chocolate mixture. Refrigerate
about 30 minutes or until set.

pears with choc-mint sauce

200g peppermint cream dark
  chocolate, chopped coarsely
¼ cup (60ml) cream
825g can pear halves in natural
  juice, drained
4 (60g) mint slice biscuits,
  chopped finely

preparation and cooking time
10 minutes
serves 4
nutritional count per serving
18.7g total fat (12.7g saturated fat);
1668kJ (399 cal); 53g carbohydrate;
3.1g protein; 3.1g fibre

1 Melt chocolate with cream in medium
heatproof bowl set over medium saucepan
of simmering water (do not let water touch
base of bowl).
2 Divide pears among serving dishes; drizzle
with sauce then sprinkle with biscuits. Serve
with ice-cream, if desired.

poached pears with port

1 large orange (300g)
2 cups (500ml) port
½ cup (110g) caster sugar
8 corella pears (480g), peeled

preparation and cooking time
1 hour (plus cooling time)
serves 4
nutritional count per serving
0.1g total fat (0g saturated fat);
1501kJ (359 cal); 55.8g carbohydrate;
0.9g protein; 2.4g fibre
If you can't find corella pears, use
beurre bosc or comice pears, instead.

1 Cut 2 x 8cm strips rind from orange. Juice orange (you need 2 tablespoons).
2 Combine port, sugar, rind, juice and 1.5 litres water in large saucepan. Add pears; bring to the boil. Reduce heat; simmer, covered, about 20 minutes or until pears are tender. Cool pears in syrup.
3 Remove pears from syrup; strain syrup into medium heatproof bowl. Return 2 cups of the strained syrup to same pan (discard remaining syrup); bring to the boil. Boil, uncovered, about 15 minutes or until syrup is reduced to about ½ cup. Serve pears drizzled with syrup.

berry mousse

2 teaspoons gelatine
2 egg whites
⅓ cup (75g) caster sugar
2 x 200g cartons low-fat
  berry-flavoured yogurt

preparation and cooking time
10 minutes (plus refrigeration time)
serves 4
nutritional count per serving
0.2g total fat (0.1g saturated fat);
686kJ (164 cal); 31.6g carbohydrate;
8.4g protein; 0g fibre

1 Sprinkle gelatine over 2 tablespoons water in small heatproof jug; place jug in small pan of simmering water, stir until gelatine dissolves, cool.
2 Beat egg whites in small bowl with electric mixer until soft peaks form. Gradually add sugar, beating until sugar dissolves.
3 Place yogurt in medium bowl; stir in gelatine mixture, fold in egg white mixture. Spoon mousse mixture into serving bowl, cover; refrigerate about 2 hours or until set. Serve mousse topped with mixed berries, if desired.

tip Famous for their delicate texture, soufflés have a reputation for being temperamental to cook (or to keep risen), but they are relatively easy to create. The key is to eat them as soon as they emerge from the oven. They will start to deflate within minutes.

tip Peach Melba was created more than a century ago by famed French chef August Escoffier at the Savoy Hotel in London, in honour of the Australian soprano Dame Nellie Melba (1861-1931). Dame Nellie reportedly loved ice cream but ate it rarely for fear that it would hurt her vocal chords.

apricot and honey soufflés

¼ cup (55g) caster sugar
4 apricots (200g)
2 tablespoons honey
4 egg whites

preparation and cooking time
45 minutes
serves 6
nutritional count per serving
0.1g total fat (0g saturated fat);
376kJ (90 cal); 19g carbohydrate;
2.6g protein; 0.6g fibre

1 Preheat oven to 180°C/160°C fan-forced. Grease six ¾-cup (180ml) soufflé dishes; sprinkle inside of dishes with a little of the sugar, place on oven tray.
2 Place apricots in small heatproof bowl, cover with boiling water; stand 2 minutes. Drain; cool 5 minutes then peel and seed apricots. Chop apricot flesh finely.
3 Combine apricot in small saucepan with remaining sugar, honey and ¼ cup water; bring to the boil. Reduce heat; simmer, uncovered, about 10 minutes or until apricots soften to a jam-like consistency.
4 Beat egg whites in small bowl with electric mixer until soft peaks form. With motor operating, gradually add hot apricot mixture, beating until just combined.
5 Divide mixture among dishes; bake 15 minutes. Dust with sifted icing sugar, if desired.

peach melba

4 medium peaches (600g)
200g fresh or thawed frozen
  raspberries
1 tablespoon icing sugar,
  approximately
500ml vanilla ice-cream

preparation and cooking time
10 minutes (plus cooling time)
serves 4
nutritional count per serving
7.7g total fat (4.8g saturated fat);
857kJ (205 cal); 22.5g carbohydrate;
4.1g protein; 4.2g fibre

1 Place 1 litre water in medium saucepan; bring to the boil. Add peaches; simmer, uncovered, 5 minutes. Remove peaches; place in bowl of cold water. When peaches are cold, remove skins.
2 Meanwhile, push raspberries through fine sieve into small bowl; sweeten pulp with sifted sugar to taste.
3 Serve peach halves with ice-cream; top with sauce, and extra raspberries, if desired.

marshmallow pavlova

4 egg whites
1 cup (220g) caster sugar
½ teaspoon vanilla extract
¾ teaspoon white vinegar

preparation and cooking time
1 hour 45 minutes
(plus cooling time)
serves 8
nutritional count per serving
0g total fat (0g saturated fat);
497kJ (119 cal); 27.6g carbohydrate;
1.8g protein; 0g fibre

1 Preheat oven to 120°C/100°C fan-forced. Line oven tray with foil; grease foil, dust with cornflour, shake away excess. Mark 18cm-circle on foil.
2 Beat egg whites in small bowl with electric mixer until soft peaks form; gradually add sugar, beating until sugar dissolves. Add extract and vinegar; beat until combined.
3 Spread meringue over circle on foil, building up at the side to 8cm in height.
4 Smooth side and top of pavlova gently. Using spatula blade, mark decorative grooves around side of pavlova; smooth top again.
5 Bake about 1½ hours. Turn off oven; cool pavlova in oven with door ajar. When pavlova is cold, cut around top edge (the crisp meringue top will fall slightly on top of the marshmallow). Pavlova can be topped with whipped cream and strawberries or your favourite fruit, if you like.

passionfruit and banana sundae

300ml thickened cream
50g mini pavlova shells,
    chopped coarsely
½ cup (125ml) passionfruit pulp
4 small bananas (520g),
    chopped coarsely

preparation and cooking time
10 minutes
serves 4
nutritional count per serving
28.2g total fat (18.4g saturated fat);
1722kJ (412 cal); 32.7g carbohydrate;
4.3g protein; 6.3g fibre

1 Beat cream in small bowl with electric mixer until soft peaks form.
2 Layer cream, pavlova pieces, passionfruit and banana among serving glasses.

baked custard

6 eggs
⅓ cup (75g) caster sugar
1 litre (4 cups) hot milk
¼ teaspoon ground nutmeg

preparation and cooking time
50 minutes
serves 6
nutritional count per serving
11.8g total fat (5.9g saturated fat);
995kJ (238 cal); 20.7g carbohydrate;
12.3g protein; 0g fibre

1 Preheat oven to 160°C/140°C fan-forced.
Grease shallow 1.5-litre (6-cup) ovenproof dish.
2 Whisk eggs and sugar in large bowl; gradually
whisk in hot milk. Pour custard mixture into
dish; sprinkle with nutmeg.
3 Place dish in larger baking dish; add enough
boiling water to come halfway up sides of dish.
Bake, uncovered, about 45 minutes. Remove
custard from baking dish; stand 5 minutes
before serving.

ice-cream with choc-peanut sauce

2 x 60g Snickers chocolate bars,
  chopped coarsely
½ cup (125ml) cream
2 tablespoons coffee-flavoured
  liqueur
1 litre (4 cups) vanilla ice-cream

preparation and cooking time
15 minutes
serves 4
nutritional count per serving
37.7g total fat (24g saturated fat);
2391kJ (572 cal); 47g carbohydrate;
8.3g protein; 2g fibre

1 Place chocolate bar and cream in small
saucepan; cook, stirring, without boiling, until
mixture is melted and sauce thickens slightly.
Remove from heat.
2 Stir in liqueur; stand 5 minutes before serving
drizzled over scoops of ice-cream.

back left: lemon lime sorbet; back right: raspberry sorbet; front: passionfruit sorbet

lemon lime sorbet

2 limes
3 lemons
1 cup (220g) caster sugar
1 egg white

preparation and cooking time
30 minutes
(plus cooling and freezing time)
serves 8
nutritional count per serving
0.1g total fat (0g saturated fat);
497kJ (119 cal); 28g carbohydrate;
0.7g protein; 0.8g fibre

1 Grate rind from limes (you need 1 tablespoon); juice limes (you need ¼ cup). Grate rind from lemons (you need 2 tablespoons); juice lemons (you need ½ cup).

2 Stir rinds, sugar and 2½ cups water in medium saucepan over high heat until sugar dissolves; bring to the boil. Reduce heat; simmer, uncovered, without stirring, 5 minutes. Transfer syrup to large heatproof jug, cool to room temperature; stir in juices.

3 Pour sorbet mixture into loaf pan, cover tightly with foil; freeze 3 hours or overnight.

4 Process mixture with egg white until smooth. Return to loaf pan, cover; freeze until firm.

passionfruit sorbet

You need 12 medium passionfruit for this recipe.

1 cup (250ml) passionfruit pulp
1 cup (220g) caster sugar
¼ cup (60ml) lemon juice
2 egg whites

preparation and cooking time
30 minutes
(plus cooling and freezing time)
serves 8
nutritional count per serving
0.1g total fat (0g saturated fat);
564kJ (135 cal); 29.5g carbohydrate;
1.4g protein; 4.4g fibre

1 Strain pulp into small bowl. Reserve seeds and juice separately.
2 Stir sugar and 2½ cups water in medium saucepan over high heat until sugar dissolves; bring to the boil. Reduce heat; simmer, uncovered, without stirring, 5 minutes. Transfer syrup to large heatproof jug, cool to room temperature; stir in lemon juice and passionfruit juice.
3 Pour sorbet mixture into loaf pan, cover tightly with foil; freeze 3 hours or overnight.
4 Process mixture with egg whites until smooth; stir in reserved seeds. Return to loaf pan, cover; freeze until firm.

raspberry sorbet

360g raspberries
1 cup (220g) caster sugar
1 tablespoon lemon juice
1 egg white

preparation and cooking time
30 minutes
(plus cooling and freezing time)
serves 8
nutritional count per serving
0.2g total fat (0g saturated fat);
556kJ (133 cal); 30.3g carbohydrate;
1g protein; 2.4g fibre

1 Press raspberries through sieve into small bowl; discard seeds.
2 Stir sugar and 2½ cups water in medium saucepan over high heat until sugar dissolves; bring to the boil. Reduce heat; simmer, uncovered, without stirring, 5 minutes. Transfer syrup to large heatproof jug, cool to room temperature; stir in raspberry pulp and lemon juice.
3 Pour sorbet mixture into loaf pan, cover tightly with foil; freeze 3 hours or overnight.
4 Process mixture with egg white until smooth. Return to loaf pan, cover; freeze until firm.

tropical fruit skewers with orange glaze

We used strawberries, bananas, pineapple and kiwifruit in this recipe. Use any tropical fruit you like.

1 large orange (300g)
2 tablespoons brown sugar
4 cups chopped mixed
   tropical fruit
200g honey-flavoured yogurt

preparation and cooking time
35 minutes
serves 4
nutritional count per serving
1.9g total fat (1.1g saturated fat);
773kJ (185 cal); 33.3g carbohydrate;
5.1g protein; 6.2g fibre

1 Grate rind from orange (you need 1 teaspoon). Juice orange (you need ¼ cup). Combine rind, juice and sugar in small saucepan; stir over low heat until sugar dissolves. Cool.
2 Preheat grill.
3 Thread fruits, alternately, onto skewers. Place skewers on oven tray lined with baking paper; pour orange mixture over skewers, coating all fruit pieces.
4 Grill skewers, turning occasionally, about 10 minutes or until browned lightly. Serve with yogurt.

Soak bamboo skewers in water for at least an hour before using, to avoid scorching and splintering during cooking.

strawberries romanoff

500g strawberries, halved
1½ tablespoons orange-flavoured
   liqueur
¼ cup (40g) icing sugar
½ cup (125ml) thickened cream

preparation and cooking time
10 minutes (plus refrigeration time)
serves 4
nutritional count per serving
11.7g total fat (7.6g saturated fat);
777kJ (186 cal); 15.3g carbohydrate;
2.8g protein; 2.8g fibre

1 Combine strawberries, liqueur and 2 tablespoons of the sifted icing sugar in large bowl; refrigerate 30 minutes. Drain strawberries over small bowl; reserve liquid. Divide three-quarters of the strawberries among serving dishes.
2 Blend or process remaining strawberries, remaining sifted icing sugar and reserved liquid until smooth. Beat cream in small bowl with electric mixer until soft peaks form; fold in strawberry mixture.
3 Top strawberries with strawberry cream.

summer fruit in blackcurrant syrup

We used apricots, plums, nectarines and peaches. Cherries and berries can also be used.

1 vanilla bean
1½ cups (375ml) blackcurrant
   syrup
1kg stone fruit, halved,
   stones removed
200g french vanilla Frûche

preparation and cooking time
30 minutes
serves 4
nutritional count per serving
3.1g total fat (1.7g saturated fat);
1480kJ (354 cal); 73.6g carbohydrate;
5g protcin; 1.3g fibre

1 Split vanilla bean in half lengthways; scrape seeds into large saucepan. Add pod, syrup and ½ cup water to pan; bring to the boil. Boil, uncovered, about 5 minutes or until syrup thickens slightly. Add fruit, reduce heat; simmer, uncovered, turning fruit occasionally, about 8 minutes or until fruit is tender.
2 Remove fruit mixture from heat; discard vanilla bean. Serve fruit and syrup topped with Frûche.

Frûche is the brand name of light, fresh French cheese (fromage frais); it has the consistency of thick yogurt with a refreshing, slightly tart taste and a smooth, creamy texture, yet is low in fat. Fruit can be served, topped with a thick yogurt, if preferred.

fresh pineapple with coconut

1 small pineapple (800g)
⅓ cup (80ml) passionfruit pulp
2 tablespoons coconut-flavoured
   liqueur
¼ cup (10g) flaked coconut,
   toasted

preparation and cooking time
10 minutes
serves 4
nutritional count per serving
1.8g total fat (1.4g saturated fat);
435kJ (104 cal); 13.6g carbohydrate;
1.8g protein; 5.3g fibre

1 Peel and core pineapple; slice thinly.
2 Divide pineapple among serving dishes; drizzle with passionfruit and liqueur, sprinkle with coconut.

baked apples

4 large Granny Smith apples
  (800g)
50g butter, melted
⅓ cup (75g) firmly packed
  brown sugar
½ cup (80g) sultanas

preparation and cooking time
1 hour
serves 4
nutritional count per serving
10.5g total fat (6.8g saturated fat);
1329kJ (318 cal); 52.1g carbohydrate;
1.2g protein; 4.3g fibre

1 Preheat oven to 160°C/140°C fan-forced.
2 Core unpeeled apples about three-quarters of the way down from stem end, making hole 4cm in diameter. Use small sharp knife to score around centre of each apple.
3 Combine remaining ingredients in small bowl. Pack sultana mixture firmly into apples; stand apples upright in small baking dish. Bake, uncovered, about 45 minutes.

chocolate mousse

200g dark eating chocolate,
  chopped coarsely
30g unsalted butter
3 eggs, separated
300ml thickened cream, whipped

preparation and cooking time
25 minutes (plus cooling and
refrigeration time)
serves 6
nutritional count per serving
34.9g total fat (21.4g saturated fat);
1777kJ (425 cal); 22.5g carbohydrate;
6.1g protein; 0.4g fibre

1 Melt chocolate in medium heatproof bowl over medium saucepan of simmering water (don't let the water touch the base of the bowl). Remove from heat; add butter, stir until smooth. Stir in egg yolks. Transfer mixture to large bowl, cover; cool.
2 Beat egg whites in small bowl with electric mixer until soft peaks form. Fold egg whites and cream into chocolate mixture, in two batches.
3 Divide mousse among serving dishes; refrigerate 3 hours or overnight. Serve with extra whipped cream, chocolate curls and fresh raspberries, if desired.

tip Granny Smith apples were cultivated in Australia in 1868 by Sydney grandmother Maria Ann ("Granny") Smith in her backyard orchard. The bright green apples are crisp, juicy and tart, which makes them versatile in cooking and perfect for baking in pies, stewing and for sauces and spreads.

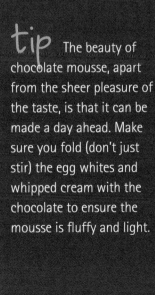

tip The beauty of chocolate mousse, apart from the sheer pleasure of the taste, is that it can be made a day ahead. Make sure you fold (don't just stir) the egg whites and whipped cream with the chocolate to ensure the mousse is fluffy and light.

toffeed mandarins with ice-cream

50g butter
⅓ cup (75g) firmly packed
  brown sugar
5 medium mandarins (1kg),
  peeled, segmented
1 litre (4 cups) vanilla ice-cream

1 Melt butter in large frying pan, add sugar and
mandarin segments; cook, stirring, until sugar
dissolves and mandarins soften slightly.
2 Divide ice-cream among serving bowls; top
with warm mandarin mixture. Serve with
almond bread, if desired.

preparation and cooking time
20 minutes
serves 4
nutritional count per serving
25.4g total fat (16.4g saturated fat);
1994kJ (477 cal); 53.8g carbohydrate;
6.6g protein; 3.6g fibre

plums with sour cream

825g can plums in syrup, drained
½ cup (120g) sour cream
½ cup (140g) honey-flavoured
  yogurt
⅓ cup (75g) firmly packed
  brown sugar

1 Halve plums; discard stones. Divide plums
among four 1-cup (250ml) shallow flameproof
serving dishes.
2 Preheat grill.
3 Combine sour cream, yogurt and 2 tablespoons
of the sugar in small bowl. Spoon sour cream
mixture over plums; sprinkle with remaining
sugar. Place under grill about 3 minutes or until
sugar dissolves.

preparation and cooking time
10 minutes
serves 4
nutritional count per serving
12g total fat (7.8g saturated fat);
1756kJ (420 cal); 74.7g carbohydrate;
1.3g protein; 2.5g fibre

roasted pear tart

1 sheet ready-rolled puff pastry
825g can pear halves in
   natural juice, drained
1 tablespoon pure maple syrup
30g butter, melted

preparation and cooking time
30 minutes

serves 4

nutritional count per serving
15.6g total fat (9.2g saturated fat);
1145kJ (274 cal); 29.2g carbohydrate;
3.1g protein; 2.6g fibre

1 Preheat oven to 200°C/180°C fan-forced.
Grease oven tray.
2 Cut pastry sheet in half; place pastry halves
about 2cm apart on prepared tray.
3 Place three pear halves, cut-side down, on
each pastry half; brush pears with combined
syrup and butter. Bake, uncovered, about
20 minutes or until pastry is puffed and
browned lightly.
4 To serve, cut in half, and accompany with
ice-cream or thickened cream, if you like.

ice-cream with espresso and irish cream

2 tablespoons finely ground
   espresso coffee
500ml vanilla ice-cream
½ cup (125ml) irish cream
   liqueur
4 chocolate-coated rolled
   wafer sticks (15g)

preparation and cooking time
15 minutes

serves 4

nutritional count per serving
13.9g total fat (9.1g saturated fat);
1099kJ (263 cal); 23.3g carbohydrate;
3.6g protein; 0g fibre

1 Place coffee and ⅔ cup boiling water in coffee
plunger; stand 2 minutes, plunge coffee. Cool
5 minutes.
2 Divide ice-cream among serving glasses; pour
liqueur then coffee over ice-cream. Serve with
wafer sticks.

We used Bailey's Irish Cream in this recipe, but
you can use any irish cream liqueur.

hot raspberry soufflés

300g frozen raspberries, thawed
½ cup (110g) caster sugar
4 egg whites
300ml thickened cream

preparation and cooking time
40 minutes
serves 4
nutritional count per serving
14.2g total fat (9.2g saturated fat);
1212kJ (290 cal); 33.3g carbohydrate;
5.3g protein; 4.1g fibre

1 Preheat oven to 180°C/160°C fan-forced. Grease four 1-cup (250ml) ovenproof dishes; place on oven tray.

2 Combine 250g of the raspberries and 1 tablespoon water in small saucepan; bring to the boil. Reduce heat; simmer, uncovered, until raspberries soften. Add sugar, stir over medium heat, without boiling, until sugar dissolves; bring to the boil. Reduce heat; simmer, uncovered, about 5 minutes or until mixture is thick and pulpy. Remove from heat; push mixture through fine sieve over small bowl, discard seeds.

3 Beat egg whites in small bowl with electric mixer until soft peaks form. With motor operating, gradually add hot raspberry mixture; beat until well combined.

4 Divide mixture among prepared dishes. Bake, uncovered, in oven, about 15 minutes or until soufflés are puffed and browned lightly.

5 Meanwhile, beat remaining raspberries and cream in small bowl with electric mixer until thickened slightly. Serve hot soufflés with raspberry cream.

crème brûlée

3 cups (750ml) thickened cream
6 egg yolks
¼ cup (55g) caster sugar
¼ cup (40g) pure icing sugar

preparation and cooking time
50 minutes (plus refrigeration time)
serves 6
nutritional count per serving
52.1g total fat (32.3g saturated fat);
2358kJ (564 cal); 19.8g carbohydrate;
5.8g protein; 0g fibre

Standing the custards in a dish
filled with ice cubes keeps them
from melting while the sugar is
caramelising under the grill.

1 Preheat oven to 180°C/160°C fan-forced.
Grease six ½-cup (125ml) ovenproof dishes.
2 Heat cream in small saucepan, without boiling.
3 Place egg yolks and caster sugar in medium
heatproof bowl; gradually whisk in hot cream.
Set bowl over medium saucepan of simmering
water (do not let the water touch the base of the
bowl); stir over heat about 10 minutes or until
custard mixture thickens slightly and coats the
back of a spoon.
4 Place prepared dishes in large baking dish;
divide custard among dishes. Add enough
boiling water to baking dish to come halfway
up sides of ovenproof dishes. Bake, uncovered,
in oven, about 20 minutes or until custard
sets. Remove custards from dish; cool. Cover;
refrigerate overnight.
5 Preheat grill. Place custards in shallow
flameproof dish filled with ice cubes; sprinkle
custards evenly with sifted icing sugar. Using
finger, spread sugar over the surface of each
custard, pressing in gently. Grill until tops of
crème brûlée caramelise.

rhubarb crumble ice-cream

2 cups (220g) coarsely
  chopped rhubarb
2 tablespoons brown sugar
2 litres vanilla ice-cream,
  softened slightly
125g Ginger Nut biscuits,
  chopped coarsely

preparation and cooking time
20 minutes (plus freezing time)
serves 8
nutritional count per serving
16.9g total fat (10.6g saturated fat);
1450kJ (347 cal); 41.9g carbohydrate;
6.2g protein; 0.9g fibre

1 Line 14cm x 21cm loaf pan with plastic wrap.
2 Cook rhubarb and sugar in large heavy-based saucepan, covered, about 5 minutes or until rhubarb is almost tender. Reduce heat; simmer, uncovered, about 5 minutes or until rhubarb softens but retains its shape. Cool.
3 Place ice-cream in large bowl; break up slightly. Gently swirl in biscuits and rhubarb mixture.
4 Pour ice-cream mixture into prepared pan. Cover; freeze 3 hours or until firm.

frozen green apple yogurt

You need a green apple weighing about 275g for this recipe.

⅓ cup (115g) honey
½ cup (125ml) apple juice
¾ cup (130g) finely grated
  unpeeled green apple
500g greek-style yogurt

preparation and cooking time
20 minutes (plus freezing time)
serves 4
nutritional count per serving
4.3g total fat (2.8g saturated fat);
896kJ (213 cal); 36.8g carbohydrate;
6.1g protein; 0.7g fibre

1 Stir honey and juice in small saucepan over low heat until honey melts; cool syrup 5 minutes.
2 Combine honey mixture, apple and yogurt in 14cm x 21cm loaf pan. Cover with foil; freeze 3 hours or overnight. Remove yogurt from freezer 15 minutes before serving.

pink grapefruit granita

1 cup (220g) white sugar
1 cup (250ml) fresh pink
  grapefruit juice
¼ cup (60ml) lemon juice
2 egg whites

preparation and cooking time
25 minutes (plus freezing time)
serves 8
nutritional count per serving
0g total fat (0g saturated fat);
526kJ (126 cal); 29.7g carbohydrate;
1.1g protein; 0g fibre

1 Stir the sugar and 1 cup water in small saucepan over heat, without boiling, until sugar dissolves. Bring to the boil; boil 5 minutes without stirring. Remove from heat; stir in juices, cool.
2 Beat egg whites in small bowl with electric mixer until soft peaks form. Fold syrup into egg white mixture; pour into 10cm x 24cm loaf pan. Cover; freeze 3 hours or overnight.
3 Blend or process granita until pale and creamy. Return to loaf pan, cover; freeze granita 3 hours or overnight.

watermelon and mint granita

1 cup (220g) white sugar
1.6kg coarsely chopped
  watermelon
2 cups firmly packed fresh
  mint leaves

preparation and cooking time
20 minutes (plus freezing time)
serves 8
nutritional count per serving
0.5g total fat (0g saturated fat);
698kJ (167 cal); 38.1g carbohydrate;
1g protein; 2.1g fibre

1 Combine sugar and 2 cups water in medium saucepan. Stir over low heat, without boiling, until sugar dissolves; bring to the boil. Reduce heat; simmer, uncovered, without stirring, about 5 minutes or until syrup thickens slightly but does not colour.
2 Blend or process watermelon and mint, in batches, until almost smooth; push batches through sieve into large bowl. Add syrup; stir to combine.
3 Pour mixture into two 20cm x 30cm lamington pans, cover with foil; freeze about 3 hours or until almost set.
4 Using fork, scrape granita from bottom and sides of pans, mixing frozen with unfrozen mixture. Cover, return to freezer. Repeat process every hour for about 4 hours or until large ice crystals form and granita has a dry, shard-like appearance. Scrape again with fork before serving.

34

Baking + Sweet Treats

From classic scones and light-as-air sponges to biscuits and melt-in-the-mouth chocolate truffles, just four ingredients is all it takes to create a favourite sweet treat for everyone.

scones

4 cups (600g) self-raising flour
2 tablespoons icing sugar
60g butter, chopped
1½ cups (375ml) milk

preparation and cooking time
45 minutes
makes 20
nutritional count per scone
3.6g total fat (2.2g saturated fat);
594kJ (142 cal); 23.2g carbohydrate;
3.6g protein; 1.1g fibre

1 Preheat oven to 220°C/200°C fan-forced. Grease 20cm x 30cm lamington pan.
2 Sift flour and icing sugar into large bowl; rub in butter with fingertips.
3 Make a well in centre of flour mixture; add milk and ¾ cup water. Use knife to "cut" the liquid through flour mixture, mixing to a soft, sticky dough. Knead dough on floured surface until smooth.
4 Press dough out to 2cm thickness. Dip 4.5cm round cutter in flour; cut as many rounds as you can from piece of dough. Gently knead scraps of dough together; repeat pressing and cutting of dough. Place scones, side by side, just touching, in pan.
5 Brush tops with a little extra milk; bake about 15 minutes or until scones are just browned and sound hollow when tapped firmly on the top with fingers. Serve warm scones with butter, or whipped cream and strawberry jam, if desired.

scottish shortbread

250g butter, chopped
½ cup (110g) caster sugar
¼ cup (35g) rice flour
2¼ cups (335g) plain flour

preparation and cooking time
20 minutes
cooking time 40 minutes
makes 16
nutritional count per shortbread
13.1g total fat (8.5g saturated fat);
936kJ (224 cal); 23.8g carbohydrate;
2.5g protein; 0.8g fibre

1 Preheat oven to 150°C/130°C fan-forced. Lightly grease two oven trays.
2 Beat butter and ⅓ cup of the sugar in medium bowl with electric mixer until light and fluffy. Stir in sifted flours, in two batches. Knead on floured surface until smooth.
3 Divide mixture in half; shape into two 20cm rounds on oven trays. Mark each round into eight wedges, prick with fork, pinch edges with fingers. Sprinkle with remaining sugar.
4 Bake about 40 minutes. Stand 5 minutes then, using sharp knife, cut into wedges along marked lines; cool on trays.

tip Devonshire tea – the classic combination of scones with jam and cream – originated in the county of Devon, in England, where it is a speciality. Nothing beats scones with jam and cream for a popular, nostalgic indulgence.

tip Don't overcook your shortbread. It should be a pale golden colour, no darker. The stiff shortbread dough retains it shape well during cooking, making it perfect for cutting into stars or other shapes for Christmas treats or other special occasions.

strawberry jelly cakes

85g packet strawberry jelly
400g bought slab sponge cake
3 cups (150g) flaked coconut
½ cup (125ml) thickened cream

preparation and cooking time
45 minutes (plus refrigeration time)
makes 36
nutritional count per cake
4.5g total fat (3.4g saturated fat);
347kJ (83 cal); 9g carbohydrate;
1.4g protein; 0.7g fibre

1 Make jelly according to directions on packet. Refrigerate until set to the consistency of unbeaten egg white.
2 Cut cake into 36 squares; dip each square into jelly then coconut. Cover; refrigerate 30 minutes.
3 Meanwhile, beat cream in small bowl with electric mixer until firm peaks form. Serve cakes with cream.

powder puffs

2 eggs
⅓ cup (75g) caster sugar
¼ cup (35g) cornflour
¼ cup (35g) self-raising flour

preparation and cooking time
35 minutes
makes 24
nutritional count per powder puff
0.5g total fat (0.1g saturated fat);
121kJ (29 cal); 5.4g carbohydrate;
0.7g protein; 0.1g fibre

1 Preheat oven to 180°C/160°C fan-forced. Grease and flour two 12-hole (1½ tablespoon/30ml) shallow round-based patty pans.
2 Beat eggs in small bowl with electric mixer until thick and creamy. Gradually add sugar, 1 tablespoon at a time, beating until sugar dissolves between additions. Sift flours together three times onto baking paper; fold into egg mixture.
3 Divide mixture among pan holes. Bake about 8 minutes. Turn immediately onto wire racks to cool.
4 If you like, serve powder puffs dusted with sifted icing sugar, or sandwich powder puffs with whipped cream and strawberries.

orange butter cookies

250g butter, softened
1 cup (160g) icing sugar
1 teaspoon finely grated
   orange rind
2½ cups (375g) plain flour

preparation and cooking time
30 minutes (plus refrigeration time)
makes 50
nutritional count per cookie
4.2g total fat (2.7g saturated fat);
318kJ (76 cal); 8.6g carbohydrate;
0.8g protein; 0.3g fibre

1 Beat butter, sifted icing sugar and rind in small bowl with electric mixer until light and fluffy. Transfer to large bowl.
2 Stir sifted flour, in two batches, into butter mixture. Knead dough on lightly floured surface until smooth. Divide dough in half; roll each half into a 25cm log. Enclose in plastic wrap; refrigerate about 1 hour or until firm.
3 Preheat oven to 180°C/160°C fan-forced.
4 Cut rolls into 1cm slices; place on greased oven trays 2cm apart. Bake about 10 minutes or until browned lightly. Turn cookies onto wire racks to cool.

maple-syrup butter cookies

125g butter, softened
⅓ cup (80ml) maple syrup
¾ cup (110g) plain flour
¼ cup (35g) cornflour

preparation and cooking time
35 minutes
makes 24
nutritional count per cookie
4.3g total fat (2.8g saturated fat);
297kJ (71 cal); 7.5g carbohydrate;
0.5g protein; 0.2g fibre

1 Preheat oven to 180°C/160°C fan-forced. Grease oven trays; line with baking paper.
2 Beat butter and maple syrup in small bowl with electric mixer until light and fluffy; stir in combined sifted flours. Spoon mixture into piping bag fitted with 1cm fluted tube.
3 Pipe stars about 3cm apart onto trays. Bake about 15 minutes; cool cookies on trays.

brown sugar sponge

4 eggs
¾ cup (165g) firmly packed
  dark brown sugar
1 cup (150g) wheaten cornflour
2 teaspoons baking powder

preparation and cooking time
40 minutes (plus cooling time)
serves 10
nutritional count per serving
2.2g total fat (0.7g saturated fat);
610kJ (146 cal); 28.5g carbohydrate;
2.7g protein; 0.1g fibre

1 Preheat oven to 180°C/160°C fan-forced. Grease two deep 22cm-round cake pans.
2 Beat eggs and sugar in small bowl with electric mixer about 10 minutes or until thick and creamy; transfer to large bowl.
3 Sift cornflour and baking powder twice onto paper then sift over egg mixture; gently fold into egg mixture. Divide mixture between pans; bake about 18 minutes. Turn sponges immediately, top-side up, onto baking-paper-covered wire racks to cool.
4 Sponge can be sandwiched with whipped cream, if desired, and dusted with sifted icing sugar.

whipped cream cake

600ml thickened cream

3 eggs

1¼ cups (275g) firmly packed brown sugar

2 cups (300g) self-raising flour

preparation and cooking time
1 hour 10 minutes
(plus cooling time)

serves 10

nutritional count per serving
24.2g total fat (15.2g saturated fat);
1856kJ (444 cal); 49.7g carbohydrate;
6.3g protein; 1.1g fibre

1 Preheat oven to 180°C/160°C fan-forced. Grease deep 22cm-round cake pan; line base with baking paper.
2 Beat half the cream in small bowl with electric mixer until soft peaks form.
3 Beat eggs in another small bowl with electric mixer until thick and creamy; gradually add sugar, beating until dissolved between additions.
4 Transfer egg mixture to large bowl. Fold in a quarter of the whipped cream then sifted flour, then remaining whipped cream. Spread into pan; bake about 50 minutes. Stand cake 5 minutes before turning, top-side up, onto wire rack to cool.
5 Meanwhile, beat remaining cream in small bowl with electric mixer until firm peaks form.
6 Split cold cake in half; sandwich layers with cream. Dust cake with sifted icing sugar, or top with caramel icing, see below, if you like.

tip To make caramel icing, melt 60g butter in a small saucepan, add ½ cup (110g) firmly packed brown sugar and 2 tablespoons milk; bring to the boil. Reduce heat immediately; simmer 2 minutes. Cool to room temperature. Stir in ½ cup (80g) sifted icing sugar until smooth.

tip You can freeze patty cakes – even with the icing on – which is handy for households with children. To thaw, just stand them at room temperature and leave for around one hour before serving them.

tip These versatile little bliss bombs can be served for morning tea, high tea or – probably best – as a post-dessert accompaniment with freshly brewed coffee.

quick-mix patty cakes

125g butter, softened
¾ cup (165g) caster sugar
3 eggs
2 cups (300g) self-raising flour

preparation and cooking time
40 minutes
makes 24
nutritional count per cake
5.1g total fat (3g saturated fat);
493kJ (118 cal); 15.7g carbohydrate;
2.1g protein; 0.5g fibre

1 Preheat oven to 180°C/160°C fan-forced.
Line two 12-hole deep flat-based patty pans
(2-tablespoons/40ml) with paper cases.
2 Combine ingredients with ¼ cup water in
medium bowl; beat with electric mixer on low
speed until ingredients are just combined. Increase
speed to medium; beat about 3 minutes or until
mixture is smooth and paler in colour.
3 Drop rounded tablespoons of mixture into
each paper case; bake about 20 minutes. Stand
cakes 5 minutes before turning, top-sides up,
onto wire racks to cool.
4 Top cakes with icing of your choice.

coffee hazelnut meringues

2 egg whites
½ cup (110g) caster sugar
2 teaspoons instant
   coffee granules
¼ cup (35g) roasted hazelnuts

preparation and cooking time
55 minutes (plus cooling time)
makes 30
nutritional count per meringue
0.7g total fat (0g saturated fat);
100kJ (24 cal); 3.7g carbohydrate;
0.4g protein; 0.1g fibre

1 Preheat oven to 120°C/100°C fan-forced.
Grease oven trays; line with baking paper.
2 Beat egg whites in small bowl with electric
mixer until soft peaks form. Gradually add sugar,
beating until dissolved between additions.
3 Meanwhile, dissolve coffee in 2 teaspoons
hot water in small jug. Fold coffee mixture into
meringue mixture.
4 Spoon mixture into piping bag fitted with
5mm fluted tube. Pipe meringues onto trays
2cm apart; top each meringue with a nut.
5 Bake about 45 minutes. Cool meringues in
oven with door ajar.

choc-peanut cornflake cookies

395g can sweetened
  condensed milk
½ cup (140g) crunchy
  peanut butter
3 cups (120g) cornflakes
80g dark chocolate Melts, melted

preparation and cooking time
45 minutes (plus standing time)
makes 26
nutritional count per cookie
5.4g total fat (2.2g saturated fat);
556kJ (133 cal); 17.2g carbohydrate;
3.5g protein; 0.8g fibre

1 Preheat oven to 200°C/180°C fan-forced.
2 Combine condensed milk, peanut butter and cornflakes in large bowl. Drop level tablespoons of mixture, 5cm apart, onto two oven trays. Bake about 12 minutes; cool on trays.
3 Drizzle cookies with chocolate; stand at room temperature until chocolate sets.

Replace the chocolate Melts with chopped dark chocolate, if preferred.

basic butter biscuits

200g butter, softened
1 cup (160g) icing sugar
1 egg
1¾ cups (260g) plain flour

preparation and cooking time
35 minutes
makes 30
nutritional count per biscuit
5.7g total fat (3.7g saturated fat);
431kJ (103 cal); 11.6g carbohydrate;
1.2g protein; 0.3g fibre

1 Preheat oven to 180°C/160°C fan-forced. Grease oven trays; line with baking paper.
2 Beat butter, sifted icing sugar and egg in small bowl with electric mixer until light and fluffy. Transfer to medium bowl; stir in sifted flour, in two batches.
3 Roll level tablespoons of dough into balls; place on trays 3cm apart. Bake about 15 minutes; cool biscuits on trays.

brandy snaps

60g butter
⅓ cup (75g) firmly packed
brown sugar
2 tablespoons golden syrup
⅓ cup (50g) plain flour

preparation and cooking time
30 minutes
makes 18
nutritional count per snap
2.8g total fat (1.8g saturated fat);
251kJ (60 cal); 8.3g carbohydrate;
0.3g protein; 0.1g fibre

1 Preheat oven to 180°C/160°C fan-forced.
Grease oven trays; line with baking paper.
2 Combine butter, sugar and syrup in small
saucepan; stir over low heat until smooth.
Remove from heat; stir in sifted flour.
3 Drop rounded teaspoons of mixture about
5cm apart on trays. Bake about 7 minutes or
until snaps bubble.
4 Slide spatula under each snap to loosen;
working quickly, wrap one snap around handle
of a wooden spoon. Remove handle; place
snap on wire rack to cool. Repeat with the
remaining snaps.
5 If you like, fill the snaps with whipped cream,
before serving.

almond macaroons

2 egg whites
½ cup (110g) caster sugar
1¼ cups (150g) almond meal
2 tablespoons plain flour

preparation and cooking time
30 minutes
makes 22
nutritional count per macaroon
3.8g total fat (0.2g saturated fat);
276kJ (66 cal); 6g carbohydrate;
1.8g protein; 0.6g fibre

1 Preheat oven to 150°C/130°C fan-forced.
Grease oven trays.
2 Beat egg whites in small bowl with electric
mixer until soft peaks form; gradually add sugar,
beating until dissolved between additions.
Gently fold in almond meal and sifted flour,
in two batches.
3 Drop level tablespoons of mixture about
5cm apart on trays; bake about 20 minutes
or until firm and dry. Cool on trays.

fruit chews

We used chopped sultanas and red glacé cherries; chopped dried apricots, pineapple or peaches can also be used.

1¼ cups (200g) mixed dried fruit
2 cups (80g) cornflakes
¾ cup (60g) roasted
 flaked almonds
⅔ cup (160ml) sweetened
 condensed milk

preparation and cooking time
15 minutes (plus standing time)
makes 25
nutritional count per chew
1.5g total fat (0.1g saturated fat);
213kJ (51 cal); 8g carbohydrate;
0.8g protein; 0.7g fibre

1 Preheat oven to 180°C/160°C fan-forced. Grease oven trays; line with baking paper.
2 Combine ingredients in medium bowl. Drop level tablespoons of mixture about 5cm apart on trays. Bake 5 minutes; cool on trays.
3 If you like, when cold, spread the bases with melted white or dark chocolate; leave at room temperature until set.

greek almond biscuits

3 cups (375g) almond meal
1 cup (220g) caster sugar
3 egg whites, beaten lightly
1 cup (80g) flaked almonds

preparation and cooking time
45 minutes
makes 25
nutritional count per biscuit
10.1g total fat (0.6g saturated fat);
619kJ (148 cal); 9.6g carbohydrate;
4.1g protein; 1.6g fibre

1 Preheat oven to 180°C/160°C fan-forced. Grease two oven trays.
2 Combine almond meal and sugar in large bowl. Add egg whites; stir until mixture forms a firm paste. Place nuts in medium shallow tray. Roll level tablespoons of the mixture through nuts; roll into 8cm logs. Shape logs to form crescents.
3 Place crescents on prepared trays; bake about 15 minutes or until browned lightly.

hedgehog slice

¾ cup (180ml) sweetened
  condensed milk
150g dark eating chocolate,
  chopped coarsely
150g plain sweet biscuits,
  chopped coarsely
⅓ cup (55g) sultanas

preparation and cooking time
15 minutes (plus refrigeration time)
serves 12
nutritional count per serving
8.4g total fat (4.5g saturated fat);
686kJ (164 cal); 19g carbohydrate;
2.7g protein; 0.6g fibre

1 Grease 8cm x 26cm bar pan; line base with
baking paper, extending paper 5cm over long
sides.
2 Combine condensed milk and chocolate in
small saucepan; stir over low heat until smooth.
3 Place biscuit pieces in large bowl with
sultanas; add chocolate mixture, stir to combine.
4 Spread mixture into pan, cover; refrigerate
about 4 hours or until firm. Remove from pan;
cut into slices.

chocolate peppermint slice

250g plain sweet biscuits
100g butter, chopped
½ cup (125ml) sweetened
  condensed milk
2 x 35g Peppermint Crisp chocolate
  bars, chopped coarsely

preparation and cooking time
15 minutes (plus refrigeration time)
makes 24
nutritional count per piece
6.3g total fat (3.9g saturated fat);
472kJ (113 cal); 12.6g carbohydrate;
1.3g protein; 0.2g fibre

1 Grease 19cm x 29cm slice pan; line base and
two long sides with baking paper, extending
paper 5cm over long sides.
2 Process 200g of the biscuits until fine. Chop
remaining biscuits coarsely.
3 Combine butter and condensed milk in small
saucepan; stir over low heat until smooth.
4 Combine processed and chopped biscuits with
chocolate bar in medium bowl; stir in butter
mixture. Press mixture firmly into pan; refrigerate,
covered, about 20 minutes or until set.
5 Cut slice into squares. Drizzle with melted
dark chocolate, if desired.

dark chocolate and ginger truffles

⅓ cup (80ml) thickened cream
200g dark eating chocolate, chopped coarsely
½ cup (115g) glacé ginger, chopped finely
¼ cup (25g) cocoa powder

preparation and cooking time
45 minutes (plus refrigeration time)
makes 30
nutritional count per truffle
3g total fat (1.9g saturated fat);
201kJ (48 cal); 4.6g carbohydrate;
0.6g protein; 0.2g fibre

1 Combine cream and chocolate in small saucepan; stir over low heat until smooth, stir in ginger. Transfer to small bowl, cover; refrigerate 3 hours or overnight.
2 Working with a quarter of the chocolate mixture at a time (keeping remainder under refrigeration), roll rounded teaspoons into balls; place on tray. Refrigerate truffles until firm.
3 Working quickly, roll truffles in sifted cocoa, return to tray; refrigerate truffles until firm.

white choc, lime and coconut truffles

½ cup (125ml) coconut cream
2 teaspoons finely grated lime rind
360g white eating chocolate, chopped coarsely
1¼ cups (85g) shredded coconut

preparation and cooking time
45 minutes (plus refrigeration time)
makes 30
nutritional count per truffle
34.8g total fat (25.5g saturated fat);
2015kJ (482 cal); 35.9g carbohydrate;
5.8g protein; 2.6g fibre

1 Combine coconut cream, rind and chocolate in small saucepan; stir over low heat until smooth. Transfer mixture to small bowl, cover; refrigerate 3 hours or overnight.
2 Working with a quarter of the chocolate mixture at a time (keeping remainder under refrigeration), roll rounded teaspoons into balls; place on tray. Refrigerate truffles until firm.
3 Working quickly, roll truffles in coconut, return to tray; refrigerate truffles until firm.

tip Chocolate truffles are a luxurious delicacy and best of all they're not hard to make, albeit a bit fiddly. Be sure to use quality ingredients (chocolate makers around the world reserve their best ingredients for their truffles) and you'll have an impressive after-dinner finale everyone will love.

tip Hand-made treats make beautiful gifts. Boxed with pretty papers these delectable little artworks are a perfect idea for a special Christmas or birthday present.

peanut butter and milk chocolate truffles

⅓ cup (80ml) thickened cream

200g milk eating chocolate, chopped coarsely

¼ cup (70g) unsalted crunchy peanut butter

¾ cup (110g) crushed peanuts

preparation and cooking time
45 minutes (plus refrigeration time)
makes 30
nutritional count per truffle
4g total fat (2g saturated fat);
247kJ (59 cal); 4.5g carbohydrate;
1.2g protein; 0.3g fibre

1 Combine cream and chocolate in small saucepan; stir over low heat until smooth, stir in peanut butter. Transfer to small bowl, cover; refrigerate 3 hours or overnight.

2 Working with a quarter of the chocolate mixture at a time (keeping remainder under refrigeration), roll rounded teaspoons into balls; place on tray. Refrigerate truffles until firm.

3 Working quickly, roll truffles in peanuts, return to tray; refrigerate truffles until firm.

coffee almond biscuits

1 tablespoon instant
coffee granules
3 cups (360g) almond meal
1 cup (220g) caster sugar
3 egg whites, beaten lightly

preparation and cooking time
30 minutes
makes 24
nutritional count per biscuit
8.3g total fat (0.5g saturated fat);
543kJ (130 cal); 9.9g carbohydrate;
3.5g protein; 1.3g fibre

1 Preheat oven to 180°C/160°C fan-forced.
Grease oven trays; line with baking paper.
2 Dissolve coffee in 2 tablespoons hot water in
large bowl; cool 5 minutes. Add almond meal,
sugar and egg whites; stir until mixture forms
a firm paste.
3 Roll level tablespoons of mixture into balls;
place on trays 3cm apart; flatten with hand.
Bake about 15 minutes; cool biscuits on trays.

turkish delight rocky road

400g white eating chocolate,
chopped coarsely
200g raspberry and vanilla
marshmallows, chopped
coarsely
200g turkish delight,
chopped finely
3/4 cup (110g) roasted unsalted
macadamias, chopped coarsely

preparation and cooking time
20 minutes (plus refrigeration time)
makes 28
nutritional count per piece
7.8g total fat (4g saturated fat);
640kJ (153 cal); 19g carbohydrate;
1.6g protein; 0.2g fibre

1 Line two 8cm x 25cm bar pans with baking
paper, extending paper 5cm over sides of pans.
2 Place chocolate in medium heatproof bowl
over medium saucepan of simmering water (do
not let water touch base of bowl). Stir until
chocolate is smooth. Cool 2 minutes.
3 Meanwhile, combine remaining ingredients
in large bowl. Working quickly, stir in chocolate;
spread mixture into pans. Refrigerate until set;
cut into 1cm slices.

34

Drinks

Whether you're looking for a detoxifying vegetable juice or a champagne cocktail, these recipes will inspire you to try a refreshing twist on your drink of choice.

caipiroska

1 lime, cut into eight wedges
2 teaspoons caster sugar
45ml vodka

preparation time 5 minutes
serves 1
nutritional count per serving
0.2g total fat (0g saturated fat);
581kJ (139 cal); 10.3g carbohydrate;
0.6g protein; 1.6g fibre

1 Using muddler (or the end of a wooden spoon),
crush lime wedges with sugar in cocktail shaker.
2 Add vodka and ½ cup crushed ice; shake
vigorously. Pour into 260ml old-fashioned glass.

cuba libre

45ml dark rum
20ml lime juice
125ml cola

preparation time 5 minutes
serves 1
nutritional count per serving
0g total fat (0g saturated fat);
623kJ (149 cal); 13.8g carbohydrate;
0.2g protein; 0g fibre

1 Place rum, juice and ½ cup ice cubes in 300ml
highball glass; stir to combine.
2 Top with cola; garnish with a lime wedge, if
you like.

tip Caipiroska is a variation of the "caipirinha", regarded as Brazil's national cocktail. The caipirinha is made with cachaça (made from sugarcane that's fermented and distilled), plus sugar and lime. Caipiroska uses vodka instead of cachaça.

tip The cuba libre (Spanish for 'free Cuba') is the original version of the "rum and coke" and is believed to have been invented in Havana around 1900. The Andrews Sisters famously recorded "Rum and Coca-Cola." in 1945, named after the drink's ingredients.

vodka martini

1 small seeded green olive, rinsed
1 tablespoon dry vermouth
45ml vodka

preparation time 5 minutes
serves 1
nutritional count per serving
0.3g total fat (0g saturated fat);
489kJ (117 cal); 0.6g carbohydrate;
0.1g protein; 0.3g fibre

1 Place olive and vermouth into chilled 120ml martini glass; swirl glass to coat in vermouth.
2 Combine vodka and 1 cup ice cubes in cocktail shaker; shake vigorously, strain into glass.

cosmopolitan

45ml vodka
30ml Cointreau
20ml cranberry juice
10ml lime juice

preparation time 5 minutes
serves 1
nutritional count per serving
0.1g total fat (0g saturated fat);
991kJ (237cal); 17.4g carbohydrate;
0.2g protein; 0g fibre

1 Combine ingredients and 1 cup ice cubes in cocktail shaker; shake vigorously.
2 Strain into chilled 230ml martini glass. Garnish with a strip of orange rind, if desired.

tom collins

60ml gin
80ml lemon juice
2 teaspoons icing sugar
80ml soda water

1 Place ingredients and ¼ cup ice cubes into chilled 340ml highball glass; stir to combine.
2 Garnish with a maraschino cherry, if desired.

preparation time 5 minutes
serves 1
nutritional count per serving
0.2g total fat (0g saturated fat);
660kJ (158 cal); 7.7g carbohydrate;
0.6g protein; 0.1g fibre

mango bellini

60ml mango nectar
15ml mango liqueur
5ml lime juice
120ml chilled brut champagne

1 Place mango nectar, liqueur and juice in chilled 230ml champagne flute; stir to combine.
2 Top with chilled champagne.

preparation time 5 minutes
serves 1
nutritional count per serving
0.1g total fat (0g saturated fat);
765kJ (183 cal); 17.2g carbohydrate;
0.6g protein; 0g fibre
Mango juice can be used instead of the mango nectar, if preferred.

coconut white russian

30ml vodka
15ml coffee-flavoured liqueur
30ml coconut-flavoured liqueur
40ml coconut cream

1 Place ingredients and ½ cup ice cubes in 180ml old-fashioned glass; stir to combine.

preparation time 5 minutes
serves 1
nutritional count per serving
10.9g total fat (8.8g saturated fat);
1379kJ (330 cal); 19.3g carbohydrate;
1.3g protein; 0.7g fibre

pink limeade

You need eight limes for this recipe.

1 cup (250ml) lime juice
½ cup (125ml) vodka
1 litre (4 cups) cranberry juice

1 Combine ingredients in large jug with 2½ cups water.
2 Cover; refrigerate until chilled.

preparation time 10 minutes
(plus refrigeration time)
makes 2 litres (8 cups)
nutritional count per 1 cup (250ml)
0.1g total fat (0g saturated fat);
435kJ (104 cal); 17.5g carbohydrate;
0.5g protein; 0.1g fibre

champagne cocktail

5cm strip orange rind
1 sugar cube
5 drops Angostura bitters
2/3 cup (160ml) chilled
   champagne

1 Slice rind thinly.
2 Place sugar cube in champagne glass; top with
bitters then champagne. Garnish with rind.

preparation time 5 minutes
serves 1
nutritional count per serving
0g total fat (0g saturated fat);
527kJ (126 cal); 6.9g carbohydrate;
0.3g protein; 0.1g fibre

moroccan mint tea

3 black tea bags
1 cup loosely packed fresh
   mint leaves
2 tablespoons caster sugar
1/2 cup loosely packed fresh
   mint leaves, extra

1 Combine tea bags, mint leaves and 1 litre hot
water in medium jug; stand 10 minutes. Discard
tea bags, cover; refrigerate until cool.
2 Strain tea mixture into medium jug; discard
leaves. Stir in sugar, extra mint leaves and 1 cup
ice cubes.

preparation time 10 minutes
(plus refrigeration time)
makes 1 litre (4 cups)
nutritional count per 1 cup (250ml)
0.5g total fat (0g saturated fat);
209kJ (50 cal); 9.8g carbohydrate;
0.8g protein; 1.4g fibre

tip This tangy, bubbly lime and lemon grass combination is a refreshing drink for outdoor summer entertaining, and a great non-alcoholic offering to have on the table during the meal.

tip This delicious, mega-healthy drink combines two super fruits – cranberries and raspberries – and there couldn't be a more pleasurable way to take in a dose of vitamin C, dietary fibre and antioxidants. And you will also be cleansing and purifying your system.

lime and lemon grass spritzer

⅓ cup (90g) grated palm sugar
2 tablespoons coarsely chopped
  fresh lemon grass
125ml lime juice
750ml chilled sparkling
  mineral water

1 Place sugar and ½ cup water in small saucepan; stir over low heat until sugar dissolves. Remove from heat; stir in lemon grass. Cover; refrigerate until chilled.
2 Combine strained sugar mixture with lime juice, mineral water and 1 cup ice cubes in large jug.

preparation and cooking time
15 minutes (plus refrigeration time)
makes 1 litre (4 cups)
nutritional count per 1 cup (250ml)
0.1g total fat (0g saturated fat);
385kJ (92 cal); 22.2g carbohydrate;
0.3g protein; 0.1g fibre

raspberry cranberry crush

500ml cranberry juice
20ml lemon juice
250ml wildberry sorbet
1 cup (150g) frozen raspberries

1 Blend or process ingredients until smooth.

preparation time 5 minutes
makes 1 litre (4 cups)
nutritional count per 1 cup (250ml)
0.2g total fat (0g saturated fat);
656kJ (157 cal); 36.2g carbohydrate;
1.2g protein; 2.1g fibre

rosemary mint camomile tea

5cm piece fresh rosemary
¼ cup loosely packed fresh
 peppermint leaves
4 camomile tea bags
1 tablespoon honey

1 Combine ingredients in large heatproof jug with 1 litre boiling water; stand 3 minutes before straining into cups or tea glasses.

preparation time 5 minutes
serves 4
nutritional count per serving
0g total fat (0g saturated fat);
105kJ (25 cal); 6.1g carbohydrate;
0.1g protein; 0.3g fibre

spiced rosehip and hibiscus tea

2 rosehip and hibiscus tea bags
2 x 10cm strips orange rind
1 cinnamon stick

1 Combine ingredients in large heatproof jug with 1 litre boiling water; stand, uncovered, 2 minutes. Strain into another large heatproof jug.

preparation time 5 minutes
serves 4
nutritional count per serving
0g total fat (0g saturated fat);
13kJ (3 cal); 0.7g carbohydrate;
0.1g protein; 0.2g fibre

lemon balm and mint cooler

1 tablespoon lemon balm tea
½ cup loosely packed fresh
   mint leaves
2 tablespoons lemon juice
2 teaspoons white sugar

preparation and cooking time
15 minutes (plus refrigeration time)
serves 4
nutritional count per serving
0.1g total fat (0g saturated fat);
59kJ (14 cal); 2.6g carbohydrate;
0.3g protein; 0.5g fibre

1 Combine tea, mint and 1 litre water in small saucepan; bring to the boil. Reduce heat; simmer, uncovered, 5 minutes. Stand 1 minute; strain into large heatproof jug.
2 Stir in juice and sugar; cool. Cover; refrigerate until cold then serve over ice.

papaya, strawberry and orange frappé

1 large papaya (1.5kg),
   coarsely chopped
250g strawberries
180ml chilled orange juice

preparation time 10 minutes
makes 1 litre (4 cups)
nutritional count per 1 cup (250ml)
0.4g total fat (0g saturated fat);
502kJ (120 cal); 23g carbohydrate;
2.3g protein; 7.4g fibre

1 Blend or process ingredients until smooth.

watermelon refresher

900g coarsely chopped seedless
watermelon
125ml chilled orange juice
40ml lime juice

1 Blend or process ingredients until smooth. Garnish with lime slices, if desired.

preparation time 10 minutes
makes 1 litre (4 cups)
nutritional count per 1 cup (250ml)
0.5g total fat (0g saturated fat);
280kJ (67 cal); 13.8g carbohydrate;
0.9g protein; 1.4g fibre

melonade

½ cup (125ml) lemon juice
2 tablespoons caster sugar
3 cups (500g) coarsely chopped
watermelon
1½ cups (375ml) chilled sparkling
mineral water

1 Combine juice and sugar in small saucepan; stir over low heat until sugar dissolves. Cool.
2 Blend or process watermelon, in batches, until smooth; strain through sieve into large jug. Stir in lemon syrup and mineral water; serve immediately.

preparation and cooking time
10 minutes (plus cooling time)
makes 1 litre (4 cups)
nutritional count per 1 cup (250ml)
0.3g total fat (0g saturated fat);
301kJ (72 cal); 16.1g carbohydrate;
0.6g protein; 0.8g fibre

kiwi and mint frappé

4 medium kiwifruit (340g),
  peeled, chopped coarsely
¼ cup (60ml) apple juice
¼ cup coarsely chopped fresh
  mint leaves
1 teaspoon caster sugar

1 Blend or process ingredients with ¾ cup ice cubes until smooth.
2 Pour into glass; top with shredded mint, if desired.

preparation time 5 minutes
serves 1
nutritional count per serving
0.8g total fat (0g saturated fat);
974kJ (233 cal); 44.8g carbohydrate;
5.2g protein; 12.2g fibre

pineapple orange frappé

1 medium pineapple (1.2kg),
  chopped coarsely
½ cup (125ml) orange juice
1 tablespoon finely grated
  orange rind

1 Blend or process pineapple and juice, in batches, until smooth.
2 Pour into large jug with rind and 3 cups crushed ice; stir to combine.

preparation time 10 minutes
makes 1 litre (4 cups)
nutritional count per 1 cup (250ml)
0.2g total fat (0g saturated fat);
339kJ (81 cal); 16g carbohydrate;
1.9g protein; 3.6g fibre

cucumber, celery, apple and spinach juice

1 telegraph cucumber (400g),
chopped coarsely
2 stalks celery (300g), trimmed,
chopped coarsely
2 large green apples (400g),
cored, chopped coarsely
50g baby spinach leaves,
stems removed

1 Process ingredients, in batches, until pureed; strain through coarse sieve into large jug.
2 Stir in 1 cup water. Refrigerate, covered, until cold.

preparation time 10 minutes
(plus refrigeration time)
makes 1 litre (4 cups)
nutritional count per 1 cup (250ml)
0.3g total fat (0g saturated fat);
255kJ (61 cal); 10.6g carbohydrate;
2g protein; 3.7g fibre

tomato, carrot and red capsicum juice

4 medium tomatoes (300g),
chopped coarsely
2 medium carrots (240g),
chopped coarsely
1 medium red capsicum (250g),
chopped coarsely
⅓ cup firmly packed fresh
flat-leaf parsley leaves

1 Process ingredients, in batches, until pureed; strain through coarse sieve into large jug.
2 Stir in 1 cup water; refrigerate until cold.

preparation time 10 minutes
(plus refrigeration time)
makes 1 litre (4 cups)
nutritional count per 1 cup (250ml)
0.2g total fat (0g saturated fat);
176kJ (42 cal); 6.3g carbohydrate;
2.1g protein; 3.2g fibre

tip Blending fruits and vegetables into a freshly squeezed juice is a wonderful source of easy-to-absorb vitamins and minerals. This combo is rich in vitamins A and C and fibre (thanks to the apples, celery and cucumber) as well as folate and magnesium from the spinach.

tip Vegetable juicing is vital to good health because it is an important source of raw food. We all need raw foods every day for optimum health, and juicing is an excellent way to satisfy the health requirements in a taste-tantilising way.

peach and raspberry juice

1 large peach (220g), peeled,
 seeded, chopped coarsely
¼ cup (35g) fresh or frozen
 raspberries

1 Process ingredients until smooth; pour
into glass.
2 Stir in ½ cup water; serve over ice.

preparation time 5 minutes
serves 1
nutritional count per serving
0.3g total fat (0g saturated fat);
314kJ (75 cal); 13.7g carbohydrate;
1.9g protein; 4.1g fibre

apple, pear and ginger juice

1 medium unpeeled apple (150g),
 cored, cut into wedges
1 medium unpeeled pear (230g),
 cored, cut into wedges
1cm piece fresh ginger (5g)

1 Push ingredients through juice extractor into
glass. Serve with ice.

preparation time 5 minutes
serves 1
nutritional count per serving
0.3g total fat (0g saturated fat);
823kJ (197 cal); 43.1g carbohydrate;
1g protein; 0.2g fibre

carrot, orange and ginger juice

1 large orange (300g), peeled,
  quartered
1 medium carrot (120g),
  chopped coarsely
1cm piece fresh ginger (5g)

1 Push ingredients through juice extractor into glass. Serve with ice.

preparation time 5 minutes
serves 1
nutritional count per serving
0.3g total fat (0g saturated fat);
506kJ (121 cal); 22.6g carbohydrate;
3g protein; 0.2g fibre

pomegranate and orange juice

2/3 cup (160ml) pomegranate pulp
2 medium oranges (480g), peeled,
  quartered

1 Push ingredients through juice extractor into glass; stir to combine.

preparation time 5 minutes
serves 1
nutritional count per serving
0.7g total fat (0g saturated fat);
1112kJ (266 cal); 49.2g carbohydrate;
6.8g protein; 17.1g fibre

cranberry cooler

1⅓ cups (150g) frozen
 cranberries, thawed
1kg watermelon, peeled,
 chopped coarsely
2 lebanese cucumbers (260g),
 chopped coarsely
2 medium pears (460g),
 chopped coarsely

1 Push ingredients through juice extractor into glass; stir to combine.

preparation time 5 minutes
makes 1 litre (4 cups)
nutritional count per 1 cup (250ml)
0.2g total fat (0g saturated fat);
134kJ (32 cal); 6.6g carbohydrate;
0.3g protein; 1.2g fibre

beetroot and silver beet juice

3 medium beetroot (525g),
 chopped coarsely
4 medium oranges (960g),
 peeled, quartered
500g trimmed silver beet
1 fresh small red thai chilli,
 chopped finely

1 Push beetroot, orange and silver beet through juice extractor into glass. Stir in 1 cup water. Add chilli; stand 5 minutes.
2 Strain mixture through fine sieve into large jug.

preparation time 5 minutes
makes 1 litre (4 cups)
nutritional count per 1 cup (250ml)
0.5g total fat (0g saturated fat);
617kJ (147 cal); 24.5g carbohydrate;
5.8g protein; 10.4g fibre

buttermilk fruit smoothie

1 small pear (180g), cored,
  chopped coarsely
1 small banana (130g),
  chopped coarsely
½ cup (125ml) chilled buttermilk
½ cup (125ml) chilled apple juice

1 Blend or process ingredients until smooth.
Pour into glass; serve over ice.

preparation time 5 minutes
serves 1
nutritional count per serving
2.8g total fat (1.7g saturated fat);
1287kJ (308 cal); 59.5g carbohydrate;
7.4g protein; 6g fibre
The smoothie can be sweetened
with honey, if you like.

strawberry smoothie

200g low-fat frozen
  strawberry yogurt
250g strawberries
1 litre (4 cups) skim milk

1 Soften yogurt slightly; cut into pieces.
Hull strawberries; cut in half.
2 Blend or process ingredients, in batches,
until smooth.

preparation time 10 minutes
serves 4
nutritional count per serving
3.5g total fat (2.3g saturated fat);
783kJ (187 cal); 27g carbohydrate;
15.6g protein; 1.4g fibre

mocha smoothie

1 litre (4 cups) skim milk
1 cup (250ml) low-fat
 chocolate mousse
1 cup (250ml) low-fat
 chocolate ice-cream
1 tablespoon instant
 coffee granules

1 Blend or process ingredients, in batches,
until smooth.

preparation time 5 minutes
serves 4
nutritional count per serving
6.9g total fat (4.6g saturated fat);
1204kJ (288 cal); 39.2g carbohydrate;
16.7g protein; 0.2g fibre

banana passionfruit soy smoothie

½ cup (125ml) passionfruit pulp
2 cups (500ml) no-fat soy milk
2 medium ripe bananas (400g),
 chopped coarsely

1 Strain pulp through sieve into small bowl;
reserve liquid and seeds separately.
2 Blend or process passionfruit liquid, milk and
banana, in batches, until smooth.
3 Pour smoothie into large jug; stir in reserved
seeds. Refrigerate, covered, until cold.

preparation time 10 minutes
(plus refrigeration time)
makes 1 litre (4 cups)
nutritional count per 1 cup (250ml)
44.7g total fat (0.5g saturated fat);
702kJ (168 cal); 21.4g carbohydrate;
6.6g protein; 6.5g fibre

ANGEL HAIR PASTA also known as barbina. Long, thin strands of pasta. Called 'capelli d'angelo' in Italian.

ANGOSTURA BITTERS used mainly in drinks. Its recipe is a closely guarded secret, but it is made of many herbs and spices.

ARROWROOT a starch used mostly for thickening. Cornflour can be substituted but will not give as clear a glaze.

BABA GHANOUSH a roasted eggplant (aubergine) dip.

BEANS
broad also known as windsor, fava and horse beans. Fresh and frozen forms should be peeled twice (discarding both the outer long green pod and the beige-green tough inner shell).
cannellini small white bean similar to great northern, navy or haricot, for which they can be substituted.
refried pinto or borlotti beans, having been cooked twice – first boiled, then mashed and fried.
white some recipes in this book may simply call for 'white beans', a generic term we use for dried or canned cannellini, haricot, navy or great northern beans.

BREAD
bagel small ring-shaped bread roll; yeast-based but egg-less, with a dense, chewy texture and shiny crust. A true bagel is boiled in water before it's baked.
brioche rich, yeast-risen french bread made with butter and eggs. Available from pâtisseries or better bakeries.
ciabatta in Italian, the word means 'slipper', which is the traditional shape of this popular white bread with a crisp crust.

english muffin made with yeast; often confused with crumpets. Pre-baked and sold packaged in supermarkets, muffins should be split open before eating.
focaccia a flat italian-style bread, also available as rolls. Made from a basic yeast dough; the top is dimpled and brushed with oil to keep the bread moist. Other toppings, such as salt or herbs, may be sprinkled on top.
french a long, narrow cylindrical loaf with a crisp crust and light chewy interior. A standard loaf is about 6cm wide and 4cm tall, but can be up to a metre long. It is also known as a french stick, french loaf or baguette.
lavash flat, unleavened bread of Mediterranean origin.
melba toasts (mini toasts) traditionally a very thin-sliced bread that has had the crusts removed before it is toasted.
mountain a soft-textured, thin, dry bread that can be used for sandwiches or rolled up and filled with numerous fillings.
pitta also known as lebanese bread. This wheat-flour pocket bread is sold in large, flat pieces that separate into two rounds.
rye made from rye flour.
sourdough so-named, not because it's sour in taste, but because it's made by using a small amount of 'starter dough', which contains a yeast culture, mixed into flour and water. Part of the resulting dough is then saved to use as the starter dough next time.
tortillas thin, round unleavened bread originating in Mexico. Two kinds are available, one made from wheat flour and the other from corn.

turkish also known as pide; comes in long (about 45cm) flat loaves as well as individual rounds. Made from wheat flour and sprinkled with sesame seeds or kalonji (black onion seeds).

BREADCRUMBS
packaged fine-textured, crunchy, purchased white breadcrumbs.
stale one- or two-day-old bread made into crumbs by blending or processing.

BROCCOLINI a cross between broccoli and chinese kale; milder and sweeter than broccoli. Each long stem is topped by a loose floret that closely resembles broccoli; from stem to floret, broccolini is completely edible.

CAJUN SEASONING a blend of herbs and spices including paprika, basil, onion, fennel, thyme, cayenne and tarragon.

CAPERS the grey-green buds of a warm climate (usually Mediterranean) shrub; sold either dried and salted or pickled in a vinegar brine. Baby capers, those picked early, are smaller, fuller-flavoured and more expensive than the full-sized ones. Capers should be rinsed well before using.

CAYENNE PEPPER see *chilli*.

CHEESE
blue brie mould-treated cheese mottled with blue veining.
bocconcini walnut-sized, fresh, baby mozzarella.
brie often referred to as the 'queen of cheeses'. Has a bloomy white rind and a smooth creamy centre that becomes runnier as it ripens.
cream cheese commonly known as Philadelphia or Philly, a soft cows-milk cheese.

edam a mellow, savoury Dutch cheese having a pale yellow interior and a red or yellow paraffin coating.

emmentaler Switzerland's oldest cheese. This cows-milk cheese is light gold in colour and has a nutty-sweet, mellow flavour. It has marble-size holes and a natural light brown rind.

fontina a smooth, firm cows-milk cheese with a nutty taste and brown or red rind; an ideal melting or grilling cheese.

gouda mild cream-coloured Dutch cheese made from cows milk. Has a mild nutty flavour.

haloumi a firm, cream-coloured sheep-milk cheese matured in brine; somewhat like a minty, salty fetta in flavour. Can be grilled or fried, briefly, without breaking down. Should be eaten while still warm as it becomes tough and rubbery on cooling.

jarlsberg a popular Norwegian cheese made from cows milk; has large holes and a mild, nutty taste.

mascarpone a buttery-rich, cream-like cheese made from cows milk. Is ivory-coloured, soft and delicate, with the texture of softened butter.

pecorino the generic Italian name for cheeses made from sheep milk. It's a hard, white to pale yellow cheese; if you can't find it, use parmesan cheese.

pizza a commercial blend of grated mozzarella, cheddar and parmesan cheeses.

CHILLI available in many types and sizes. Use rubber gloves when seeding and chopping fresh chillies as they can burn your skin. Removing seeds and membranes lessens the heat level.

cayenne pepper thin-fleshed, long, extremely hot, dried red chilli, usually purchased ground.

flakes deep-red, dehydrated chilli slices and whole seeds.

green any unripened chilli; also some varieties that are ripe when green, such as jalapeño, habanero, poblano or serrano.

long red available both fresh and dried; a generic term used for any moderately hot, long (about 6-8cm long), thin chilli.

red thai also known as 'scuds'; small, bright red and very hot.

CHINESE BARBECUED DUCK traditionally cooked in special ovens, this duck has a sweet-sticky coating made from soy sauce, sherry, five-spice and hoisin sauce. It is available from Asian food stores.

CHOCOLATE

chocolate-hazelnut spread we use Nutella; developed during World War 2 when chocolate was in short supply – hazelnuts were added to the chocolate to increase supply.

dark chocolate peppermint cream a confectionary with a peppermint fondant centre that is covered in dark chocolate.

Melts discs of compounded dark chocolate ideal for melting and moulding.

CHORIZO made of coarsely ground pork and seasoned with garlic and chilli.

CORELLA PEAR miniature dessert pear up to 10cm long.

CORIANDER when fresh is also known as pak chee, cilantro or chinese parsley; a green-leafed herb with a pungent flavour. Also available ground or as seeds; cannot be substituted for fresh.

COUSCOUS a fine, grain-like cereal product made from semolina. A semolina dough is sieved then dehydrated to produce minuscule pellets of couscous; it is rehydrated by steaming, or with the addition of a warm liquid, and swells to three or four times its original size.

CREAM we use fresh cream, also known as pure cream and pouring cream.

crème fraîche mature fermented cream with a slightly tangy, nutty flavour and velvety texture.

CUCUMBER

lebanese short, slender and thin-skinned. Probably the most popular variety because of its tender, edible skin, tiny, yielding seeds and sweet, fresh taste.

telegraph also known as the european or burpless cucumber; slender and long (35cm), its thin dark-green skin has shallow ridges running down its length.

DUKKAH SPICE MIXTURE an Egyptian specialty made up of roasted nuts, seeds and an array of aromatic spices.

FIRM WHITE FISH FILLET blue eye, bream, flathead, ling, swordfish, whiting, jewfish, snapper or sea perch are all good choices. Check for small pieces of bone in the fillets and use tweezers to remove them.

GAI LAN also known chinese broccoli, gai larn, kanah, gai lum and chinese kale; appreciated more for its stems than its coarse leaves.

GHEE clarified butter with the milk solids removed; this fat can be heated to high temperatures without burning.

GINGER known as green or root ginger; the thick root of a tropical plant.

GOLDEN SYRUP a by-product of refined sugar cane; pure maple syrup or honey can be substituted.

HARISSA see pastes.

HORSERADISH CREAM a commercially prepared creamy paste made of vinegar, oil, sugar and grated horseradish. Not the same as prepared horseradish, which is preserved grated horseradish root.

HUMMUS a Middle-Eastern salad or dip made from garlic, chickpeas, lemon juice and tahini (sesame seed paste).

KAFFIR LIME LEAVES also known as bai magrood. Looks like two glossy dark green leaves joined end to end, forming a rounded hourglass shape; used similarly to bay leaves. A strip of fresh lime peel may be substituted for each kaffir lime leaf.

KECAP MANIS see sauces.

KITCHEN STRING made of a natural product, such as cotton or hemp, so it neither affects the flavour of the food it's tied around nor melts when heated.

KUMARA name of an orange-fleshed sweet potato often confused with yam.

LAMINGTON PAN 20cm x 30cm slab cake pan, 3cm deep.

LEMON PEPPER SEASONING a blend of crushed black pepper, lemon, herbs and spices.

LENTILS (red, brown, yellow) dried pulses often identified by and named after their colour.

MALIBU coconut-flavoured rum.

MIRIN sweet rice wine used in Japanese cooking; not to be confused with sake.

MIXED SALAD LEAVES mixed baby leaves, also sold as salad mix, mesclun or gourmet salad mix; a mix of assorted young lettuce and other green leaves.

MIZUNA a wispy, feathered green salad leaf.

MORTADELLA a cured sausage made of ground pork that is mashed into a paste then flavoured with spices.

MUDDLER a bartender's tool, used to crush or mash, fruits, herbs, and/or spices in the bottom of a glass to release their flavour. Use the end of a small rolling pin or thick wooden spoon handle, or a pestle, if you don't have one.

MUSHROOMS
oyster also known as abalone; grey-white mushrooms shaped like a fan. Has a smooth texture and subtle, oyster-like flavour.
shiitake, fresh are also known as chinese black, golden oak or forest mushrooms. Although cultivated, they are large and meaty and have the earthiness and taste of wild mushrooms.
swiss brown also known as roman or cremini. Light to dark-brown mushrooms with a full-bodied flavour.

ONION
green also known as scallion or, incorrectly, shallot; an immature onion picked before the bulb has formed, having a long, bright-green edible stalk.
pickling or cocktail onions; are baby brown or white onions.
red also known as spanish, red spanish or bermuda onion.

shallots also called french shallots, golden shallots or eschalots; small, brown-skinned, elongated members of the onion family.

PALM SUGAR also known as nam tan pip, jaggery, jawa or gula melaka; made from the sap of the sugar palm tree. Light brown to black in colour and usually sold in rock-hard cakes. Substitute with brown sugar if unavailable.

PANCETTA an Italian unsmoked bacon; pork belly is cured in salt and spices then rolled into a sausage shape and dried.

PAPAYA also known as pawpaw or papaw; large, pear-shaped red-orange tropical fruit. Can also be used unripe (green) in Asian cooking.

PARSLEY FLAT-LEAF also known as continental or italian parsley.

PASTES
harissa a moroccan paste made from dried chillies, cumin, garlic, oil and caraway seeds; available from Middle-Eastern food stores and some supermarkets.
red curry probably the most popular curry paste; a medium heat blend of chilli, garlic, onion, lemon grass, spice and galangal.
tandoori a medium heat paste consisting of garlic, tamarind, ginger, coriander, chilli and other spices.
tikka a medium/mild paste consisting of chilli, coriander, cumin, lentil flour, garlic, ginger, turmeric, fennel, pepper, cloves, cinnamon and cardamom.
yellow curry one of the mildest pastes; similar to Indian curry paste due to the use of mild yellow chilli and fresh turmeric.

PEKING DUCK PANCAKES
small, round crepes or pancakes made with plain flour; they can be purchased commercially in Asian food stores. To prepare pancakes, place in a steamer set over a large pan of simmering water. Steam about 5 minutes or until warm and pliable.

PEPPERCORNS
canned green soft, under-ripe berry preserved in brine and sold in cans. It has a fresh flavour that's less pungent than the berry in its other forms.
peppercorns, mixed dried a mix of dried pink, white and black peppercorns.

PEPPERMINT CRISP a chocolate bar with a crisp peppermint centre covered with chocolate.

PIZZA BASES pre-packaged for home-made pizzas. Come in a variety of sizes (snack or family) and thicknesses (thin and crispy or thick); some are already coated with tomato paste.

POLENTA also known as cornmeal; a flour-like cereal made of dried corn (maize) and sold ground in different textures. Also the name of the dish made from it.

POMEGRANATE fruit of a large bush native to the Middle-East, although it is now grown in other regions around the world. A dark-red, leathery-skinned fruit about the size of an orange filled with hundreds of seeds (pulp), each wrapped in an edible lucent-crimson jelly-like pulp having a tangy sweet-sour flavour.

POTATOES
desiree a long oval potato with smooth pink skin and firm pale-yellow flesh; good for baking.

king edward a plump and rosy potato; creamy when mashed.
lasoda a round, red-skinned potato with deep eyes and a white flesh; good for mashing.
nadine oval-shaped with smooth white skin and firm creamy coloured flesh; good in salads.
russet burbank also known as idaho. Reddish brown in colour and good for baking and frying.
sebago an oval, white-skinned potato; good for mashing.

PROSCIUTTO unsmoked Italian ham; salted, air-cured and aged, it is usually eaten uncooked.

QUAIL small, delicate flavoured, domestically grown game bird ranging in weight from 250g to 300g; also known as partridge.

REDCURRANT JELLY a preserve made from redcurrants; used as a glaze or in sauces.

RICE
arborio small round-grain rice; well suited to absorb a large amount of liquid, especially good in risottos.
basmati a white, fragrant long-grained rice. Wash several times before cooking.
doongara a white rice with a lower glycaemic index (GI) than most other rices, so it is more slowly absorbed into the blood stream, providing sustained energy release for endurance. Cooks to a firm, fluffy rice, even if it is overcooked.
jasmine a fragrant long-grained white rice; long-grain white rice can be substituted, but will not taste the same.
long-grain white elongated grain, remains separate when cooked; most popular steaming rice in Asia.

RICE PAPER SHEETS also known as banh trang. Made from rice paste and stamped into rounds. Are quite brittle and will break if dropped; dipped momentarily in water they become pliable wrappers.

ROCKET also known as arugula, rugula and rucola; a peppery-tasting green leaf. Baby rocket leaves, also known as wild rocket, are smaller and less peppery.

SAFFRON THREADS available in strands or ground form; imparts a yellow-orange colour to food once infused. Quality varies greatly; the best is the most expensive spice in the world. Store in the freezer.

SALAMI cured sausages heavily seasoned with garlic and spices.

SAUCES
barbecue spicy, tomato-based sauce used to marinate, baste or as an accompaniment.
béchamel also known as white sauce; a term for white or blond sauces. In its simplest form it is made from butter, flour and milk.
char siu a Chinese barbecue sauce made from sugar, water, salt, fermented soya bean paste, honey, soy sauce, malt syrup and spices. It can be found at most supermarkets.
cranberry a packaged product made of cranberries cooked in sugar syrup.
hoisin a thick, sweet and spicy Chinese paste made from salted fermented soya beans, onions and garlic.
kecap manis a dark, thick sweet soy sauce. The sweetness is derived from the addition of either molasses or palm sugar when brewed.

oyster Asian in origin, this rich, brown sauce is made from oysters and their brine, cooked with salt and soy sauce, and thickened with starches.

piri-piri (peri-peri) the hot West African sauce made from dried and soaked piri-piri chillies. Is available in bottles from delis and supermarkets.

plum a thick, sweet and sour dipping sauce made from plums, vinegar, sugar, chillies and spices.

soy made from fermented soya beans. Several variations are available in most supermarkets and Asian food stores.

japanese soy is an all-purpose low-sodium soy sauce made with more wheat content than its Chinese counterparts. Possibly the best table soy, and the one to choose if you only want one variety.

light soy is a fairly thin, pale, salty tasting sauce; used in dishes where the natural colour of the ingredients is to be maintained. Not to be confused with salt-reduced or low-sodium soy sauces.

sweet chilli a reasonably mild sauce made from red chillies, sugar, garlic and vinegar.

tamari a thick, dark sauce made mainly from soya beans. Has a mellow flavour. Available from Asian food stores.

tomato also known as ketchup or catsup; made from tomatoes, vinegar and spices.

tomato pasta made from herbs, tomatoes and spices.

worcestershire a dark-brown, thin, spicy sauce made from anchovies, tamarind, molasses and other seasonings.

SILVER BEET also known as swiss chard, blettes and, mistakenly, spinach.

SNOW PEAS also called mange tout; a variety of garden pea, eaten pod and all.

SOY MILK a rich creamy 'milk' extracted from soya beans that have been crushed in hot water and strained. Has a nutty flavour.

SPINACH also known as english spinach and, incorrectly, silver beet.

STAR ANISE a dried star-shaped fruit of a tree native to China. The pods have an astringent aniseed or licorice flavour. Available whole and ground, it is an essential ingredient in five-spice powder.

SUMAC a purple-red, astringent spice ground from berries growing on shrubs that flourish wild around the Mediterranean; adds a tart, lemony flavour to meats and dips. Available from Middle-Eastern food stores.

TABBOULEH a Middle-Eastern dish made with bulgur wheat, tomatoes, onions, parsley, mint, olive oil and lemon juice.

TAHINI a rich sesame-seed paste available from Middle-Eastern food stores; most often used in hummus, baba ghanoush and other Lebanese recipes.

TAMARI *see sauces.*

TAMARIND a sweet-sour, slightly astringent paste made from the viscous pulp of the seeds of the tamarind tree; can be dried and pressed into the blocks found in Asian food shops.

TURMERIC also known as kamin; known for the golden colour it imparts to the dishes of which it's a part.

VANILLA BEAN dried long, thin pod from a tropical golden orchid; the tiny black seeds impart a luscious vanilla flavour.

VINEGAR

balsamic made from the juice of Trebbiano grapes; is a deep rich brown colour with a sweet and sour flavour.

cider (apple cider) made from fermented apples.

malt (brown malt) made from fermented malt and beech shavings.

red wine based on fermented red wine.

rice a colourless vinegar made from fermented rice, sugar and salt. Also known as seasoned rice vinegar.

rice wine made from rice wine lees (the sediment left after fermentation), salt and alcohol.

white made from spirit of cane sugar.

white wine made from white wine.

WASABI an Asian horseradish sold as a powder or paste. Has a hot, pungent taste.

WATERCRESS also known as winter rocket; a peppery green. Highly perishable, so use as soon as possible after purchase.

WITLOF also known as chicory or belgian endive. Cigar-shaped, with tightly packed heads and pale, yellow-green or burgundy tips. Has a delicate bitter flavour.

ZA'ATAR a blend of whole roasted sesame seeds, sumac and crushed dried herbs, such as wild marjoram and thyme; its content is largely determined by each individual maker. It is available from Middle-Eastern and specialty food stores.

Measures

One Australian metric measuring cup holds approximately 250ml; one Australian metric tablespoon holds 20ml; one Australian metric teaspoon holds 5ml.

The difference between one country's measuring cups and another's is within a two- or three-teaspoon variance, and will not affect your cooking results. North America, New Zealand and the United Kingdom use a 15ml tablespoon.

All cup and spoon measurements are level. The most accurate way of measuring dry ingredients is to weigh them. When measuring liquids, use a clear glass or plastic jug with metric markings.

We use large eggs with an average weight of 60g.

Dry Measures

METRIC	IMPERIAL
15g	½oz
30g	1oz
60g	2oz
90g	3oz
125g	4oz (¼lb)
155g	5oz
185g	6oz
220g	7oz
250g	8oz (½lb)
280g	9oz
315g	10oz
345g	11oz
375g	12oz (¾lb)
410g	13oz
440g	14oz
470g	15oz
500g	16oz (1lb)
750g	24oz (1½lb)
1kg	32oz (2lb)

Liquid Measures

METRIC	IMPERIAL
30ml	1 fluid oz
60ml	2 fluid oz
100ml	3 fluid oz
125ml	4 fluid oz
150ml	5 fluid oz (¼ pint/1 gill)
190ml	6 fluid oz
250ml	8 fluid oz
300ml	10 fluid oz (½ pint)
500ml	16 fluid oz
600ml	20 fluid oz (1 pint)
1000ml (1 litre)	1¾ pints

Length Measures

METRIC	IMPERIAL
3mm	⅛in
6mm	¼in
1cm	½in
2cm	¾in
2.5cm	1in
5cm	2in
6cm	2½in
8cm	3in
10cm	4in
13cm	5in
15cm	6in
18cm	7in
20cm	8in
23cm	9in
25cm	10in
28cm	11in
30cm	12in (1ft)

Oven Temperatures

These oven temperatures are only a guide for conventional ovens. For fan-forced ovens, check the manufacturer's manual.

	°C (CELSIUS)	°F (FAHRENHEIT)	GAS MARK
Very slow	120	250	½
Slow	150	275-300	1-2
Moderately slow	160	325	3
Moderate	180	350-375	4-5
Moderately hot	200	400	6
Hot	220	425-450	7-8
Very hot	240	475	9

A

B

C

TEST KITCHEN
Food director Pamela Clark
Food editor Cathie Lonnie
Nutritional information Belinda Farlow

ACP BOOKS
General manager Christine Whiston
Editorial director Susan Tomnay
Creative director Hieu Nguyen
Designers Hannah Blackmore, Caryl Wiggins
Senior editor Wendy Bryant
Director of sales Brian Cearnes
Marketing manager Bridget Cody
Business analyst Rebecca Varela
Operations manager David Scotto
Production manager Victoria Jefferys
International rights enquiries Laura Bamford
lbamford@acpuk.com

ACP Books are published by ACP Magazines
a division of PBL Media Pty Limited
Group publisher, Women's lifestyle Pat Ingram
Director of sales, Women's lifestyle Lynette Phillips
Commercial manager, Women's lifestyle Seymour Cohen
Marketing director, Women's lifestyle Matthew Dominello
Public relations manager, Women's lifestyle Hannah Deveraux
Creative director, Events, Women's lifestyle Luke Bonnano
Research Director, Women's lifestyle Justin Stone
ACP Magazines, Chief Executive officer Scott Lorson
PBL Media, Chief Executive officer Ian Law

Cover Rigatoni marinara, page 77
Photographer Stuart Scott
Stylist Kate Brown
Photochef Belinda Farlow

Produced by ACP Books, Sydney.
Published by ACP Books, a division of ACP Magazines Ltd,
54 Park St, Sydney; GPO Box 4088, Sydney, NSW 2001
phone (02) 9282 8618 fax (02) 9267 9438.
acpbooks@acpmagazines.com.au
www.acpbooks.com.au
Printed in China through Phoenix Offset.
Australia Distributed by Network Services,
phone +61 2 9282 8777 fax +61 2 9264 3278
networkweb@networkservicescompany.com.au
United Kingdom Distributed by Australian Consolidated Press (UK),
phone (01604) 642 200 fax (01604) 642 300 books@acpuk.com
New Zealand Southern Publishers Group, 21 Newton Road,
Newton, Auckland.
phone (64 9) 360 0692 fax (64 9) 360 0695 hub@spg.co.nz
Canada Distributed by Publishers Group Canada
phone (800) 663 5714 fax (800) 565 3770
service@raincoast.com
South Africa Distributed by PSD Promotions,
phone (27 11) 392 6065/6/7 fax (27 11) 392 6079/80
orders@psdprom.co.za

Title: Just four ingredients:
the Australian women's weekly/food director, Pamela Clark.
ISBN: 978 1 86396 848 5 (pbk.)
Subjects: Quick and easy cookery.
Other Authors/Contributors: Clark, Pamela.
Also Titled: Australian women's weekly.
Dewey Number: 641.5

© ACP Magazines Ltd 2008
ABN 18 053 273 546
This publication is copyright. No part of it may be reproduced
or transmitted in any form without the written permission
of the publishers.

To order books, phone 136 116 (within Australia).
Send recipe enquiries to: askpamela@acpmagazines.com.au